The Black Mirror

**An Eastern Orthodox Look at the Dark
Side of Technology and Its Best Use**

Volume 6: Dissertations

C.J.S. Hayward

C.J.S. Hayward Publications   Spotsylvania

You are invited to visit the author website at
https://cjshayward.com, and explore other, related titles on
his bookshelf at https://cjshayward.com/books/.

To Avery Coonley School,
which provided me a good home to venture out from—
Many thanks!

Table of Contents

Foreword to the
The Black Mirror series

I gave my heirarch and abbot a copy of *The Luddite's Guide to Technology* for Christmas, and told him, "If I've contributed something to the conversation, it's probably in this book."

This collection is intended to break the contents of that book and a few related works into smaller and more manageable volumes, and give an introduction and discussion questions for individual works.

My life as a whole has been heavy with technology and heavy with theology / patrology, and my distinctive contributions may lie in relation to both. It's very easy to have your life taken over and run by technology; this is about unplugging to an extent, mastering the technologies you use, and using technologies so that they are beneficial instead of draining you. The reality is that without a conscious effort, and perhaps with many kinds of conscious effort, you will be hit by the dark sides of technology.

If this series succeeds, it will be relevant both when it was written, and later on when there are some of the same kinds of forces at play but the list of technologies that are *au courant* has shifted in significant ways.

I do not wish to continue to update this series to continue to give the impression that it was just written, but there is something timeless even to good books on technology. As regards television, I unhesitatingly draw on Neil Postman's 1985 *Amusing Ourselves to Death: Public Discourse in an Age of Show Business*,[1] Jerry Mander's 1978 *Four Arguments for the **Elimination** of Television*,[2] and Marie Winn's 1977 *The Plug-in Drug*[3] as worth listening to today. None of them anticipate ubiquitous mobile devices, and Jerry Mander is skeptical about whether computers would be of any real use for consumers. I don't mean that Mander was skeptical about whether personal-use computers would be an overall improvement to the picture; I mean that he did not anticipate personally owned computers or computer networks at all, let alone mobile Internet devices. But when you read one of his arguments, the argument of "artificial unusualness,"[4] under "Argument Four: The Inherent Biases of Television,"[5] a relatively light edit could give the impression of an incisive analysis of technology—*today*—whose ink is still wet on its pages. *Artificial unusuality was part of television when he wrote it, it is more a part of television now, it is a feature of social media, and it is a core part to how you make technology addictive today.*[6] It is not just because I have

[1] Neil Postman, *Amusing Ourselves to Death: Public Discourse in the Age of Showbusiness* (London: Methuen, 2007).

[2] Jerry Mander, *Four Arguments for the Elimination of Television* (New York: Perennial, 2002).

[3] Marie Winn, *The Plug-in Drug* (New York: Penguin, 1985).

[4] Jerry Mander, *Four Arguments for the Elimination of Television* (New York: Perennial, 2002), 299-322.

[5] Jerry Mander, *Four Arguments for the Elimination of Television* (New York: Perennial, 2002), 263-346.

[6] See, for instance, "The Acceleration of Addictiveness," The acceleration of

heard people say that television is the future of the Internet that I believe these books about technology are relevant. Much may have changed in the intervening 40-50 years since Mander wrote his title, but *the more some things change, the more some things stay the same*. The principles in these precursors to this series are still relevant, and I believe the principles in this collection will likely be at least partially relevant when smartphones and smartwatches are no longer the cutting edge of mainstream consumer use of technology, and, perhaps, there will seem to be something quaint about the concept of watching porn on a flat and external screen.

When I first wrote " 'Social Antibodies' Needed: A Request of Orthodox Clergy" (in volume 4 of this series)[7] in 2014, I made multiple attempts at a literature search on Amazon found nothing much on some other queries, and "orthodox technology" turned up, among Orthodox Christian works on technology: my own work and nobody else's.

At the time of this writing that is no longer true. The first result for that search is no longer one of my own: *Religion, Science, and Technology*.[8] Jean-Claude Larchet's *The New Media Epidemic: The Undermining of Society, Family, and Our Own Soul*[9] is on Amazon now and eminently worth reading. But my own works represent six

addictiveness, accessed November 18, 2022, http://www.paulgraham.com/addiction.html.

[7] C.J.S. Hayward, *The Black Mirror: An Eastern Orthodox Look at the Dark Side of Technology and Its Best Use: Volume 4: Nitty, Gritty, Ascesis*, Spotsylvania: C.J.S. Hayward Publications, 2024.

[8] Katina Michael, M. G. Michael, and Kallistos, *Religion, Science & Technology: An Eastern Orthodox Perspective ; an Interview with Metropolitan Kallistos Ware* (Wollongong, Australia: University of Wollongong, 2017).

[9] Jean-Claude Larchet and Archibald Andrew Torrance, *The New Media Epidemic: The Undermining of Society, Family, and Our Own Soul* (Jordanville, NY: Holy Trinity Publications, The Printshop of St Job of Pochaev, Holy Trinity Monastery, 2019).

of the first page Amazon search results for that query. As I said in " 'Social Antibodies' Needed," about what I found when I searched Amazon, *"Um, **thanks**, I think. I guess I'm an expert, or at least a resource, and even if I didn't want to, I should probably make myself available to Orthodox clergy, with my spiritual father and bishop foremost."* But for the most part, I am a somewhat obscure local expert if I am in fact a local subject-matter expert.

There may be a number of things I fail to project about the practical realities of the Internet of Bodies but I suspect this book, an attempt at outlining Orthodox ascesis governing technology use, will be somewhere on the scene then. There are some technologies that I have avoided using at all on overpowering negative intuitions, like SecondWife, er, SecondLife, and recommendations may shift from "Use freely," to "Use carefully," to "Use very cautiously," to "Better not to use," to "Don't use at all." We are having more concentrated versions of earlier precursors today, like eighty proof liquor followed age-old wine in ages past. And the case for abstinence may grow increasingly strong as the list of technologies that are *au courant* grows increasingly strong.

So you have in your hands something that may turn out to be significant, possibly moreso than my Amazon reviews may reflect. (After I posted a critique of the "Blessed Seraphim Rose" crowd,[10] admirers were not sated by giving that specific work one star reviews. They also follow through to see that positive Amazon ratings and reviews of any of my works continue to be taken down if they can be dislodged. This may also be part of why my works get one star reviews simply alleging, in two words, "Poorly written."[11])

[10] C.J.S. Hayward, *The Seraphinians: "Blessed Seraphim Rose" and His Axe-Wielding Western Converts* (Wheaton, IL: C.J.S. Hayward Publications, 2012).
[11] "Amazon.com: The Luddite's Guide to Technology: The Past Writes Back to Humane Tech!," Amazon, accessed November 18, 2022,

Reading Marie Winn's *The Plug-in Drug*[12] helped me appreciate why my political science professor at Calvin forcefully told a class, "*Playboy* is more Christian than *Sesame Street*![13]" I am writing at a time when technologies are addictive and need to be carefully used if they are used at all, and works like "The Acceleration of Addictiveness" (at https://paulgraham.com/addiction.html)[14] suggest that such caution will only be more thoroughly justified as time continues and further modifications of technology unfold before us.

Why Orthodoxy?

One Orthodox community member talked about how he asked people, "I want to understand Orthodoxy. What books should I read?" He got an answer of, "You don't understand Orthodoxy by reading a book. You understand Orthodoxy by attending services." And that is how he answers requests other people make of him for reading recommendations to understand Orthodoxy.

Orthodoxy is an oral culture that uses reading, and monasticism more so. This book is not intended to explain Orthodoxy; you must attend Orthodox services if you want that. But Orthodoxy is how I understand being human and Orthodox theology has "Who are we?" for one of the biggest

---

https://www.amazon.com/Luddites-Guide-Technology-Writes-Humane/dp/1731439539.

[12] Marie Winn, *The Plug-in Drug* (New York: Penguin, 1985).

[13] I believe his reason this forceful and possibly exaggerated statement is that *Playboy* is an open and undisguised evil that young people are warned about; *Sesame Street* is a whitewashed tomb full of rotten things which masquerades as a messenger of all things good, wholesome, and educational, and that is a bigger mark of the satanic. ("And no marvel; for Satan himself masquerades as an angel of light," 2 Corinthians 11:14, *Classic Orthodox Bible*.)

[14] "The Acceleration of Addictiveness," The acceleration of addictiveness, accessed November 18, 2022, http://www.paulgraham.com/addiction.html.

questions to answer.[15] This big question includes another capitally important question: "What is good for us as human beings?" This in turn includes "What use and abstention from technology is good for us as human beings?" That question drives this whole series. I do not write to reason you into being Orthodox, but I would be mistreating you to use anything less than the best resources I know to answer the challenges of technology and using technology without burning yourself.

Electronic technology has perhaps been around for a couple hundred years or less.[16] Our genus *Homo* has been around for millions of years,[17] and our subspecies *Homo sapiens sapiens* has been around for over a hundred thousand years.[18] This means that for well over 99% of the time our human race has been around, electronic technology was simply not part of the picture for anyone. *Maybe the keys to human flourishing and the conditions that the human person are adapted to, are older than electronic technology, and perhaps there are things we need to learn from what was normal human life.*
Let's go!

[15] When I was beginning studying theology at Cambridge in 2002, in an early tutorial supervision I was told that the three fundamental questions in theology are "Who is God?", "Who are we?", and "How do we relate to God?"
[16] "History of Technology Timeline," Encyclopædia Britannica (Encyclopædia Britannica, inc.), accessed November 18, 2022, https://www.britannica.com/story/history-of-technology-timeline.
[17] "Homo," Wikipedia (Wikimedia Foundation, November 7, 2022), https://en.wikipedia.org/wiki/Homo.
[18] Glenn Elert, "Age of Homo Sapiens," Age of Homo Sapiens - The Physics Factbook, accessed November 18, 2022, https://hypertextbook.com/facts/1997/TroyHolder.shtml.

Foreword to *Scholarly Works*

I no longer consider myself a scholar, and am working to grow into being a monk and repent of my sins for the rest of my life.

However, I received a significant scholarly formation, and the imprint of that scholarship is on my works.

This volume comprises one dissertation in pure mathematics, and two dissertations in academic theology, one written shortly before I joined the Orthodox Church and the other shortly after. They are both in relation to "religion and science," but in opposite ways, the first drawing on concepts used in computer science, and the second offering a critique of something in computer science. The trajectory from STEM to theology is one that is significant, and I believe nothing is wasted; all of them laid the grounding for my signal contribution as is meant to be showcased in this series.

Math **is** hard; Einstein said, "Do not worry about your difficulties with mathematics. I can assure you that mine are greater still. Non-technical readers might skip or skim the math thesis, but it is my hope that readers in the humanities would be able to take at least something from both of the latter two dissertations.

Note on Footnotes and Claim to Originality

It has been a thing to want originality, and to footnote debts to other authors but otherwise at least implicitly claim, "Except as I explicitly document otherwise, I was born in a house that I built with my own two hands."

There may be some original content in my writing, even strikingly original and possibly groundbreaking, but the claim I make to originality is nil. I have many debts to many people and more than I can trace (such may be classified as "unintentional plagiarism"), and I do not believe I was born in a house I built with my own two hands. I attempt the renovation and expansion of a mansion whose first roots I cannot trace and which has been touched by many hands before me, and God willing will be touched by many hands after.

When I was an aspiring scholar with an academic library, and I had an essay or assignment, I would do a literature search among the scholarly literature, and document what were often genuine dependencies and my genuine sources. That is not my situation now. *That is not the situation of my readers now.* I made footnotes for the book the first volume in this series was largely drawn from, and what I found was that I was doing five minute Googlepedia hits that may have documented a claim but generally had nothing to do with where I got my ideas. And today, when in the title of one book I would probably like, we are *Amusing and Informing Ourselves to Death*, people carry cellphones and those who trace a footnote are probably about as capable as I am of a five minute Googlepedia hit.

Additionally, this work as it originally stands has a little more than a thousand pages of various kinds of un-footnoted writing. If we say that comes with an average of three footnotes per page and five minutes per footnote, that comes to over fifteen thousand footnotes, taking more than two hundred and fifty hours, or more than six uninterrupted forty hour workweeks. And I hardly have forty hour workweeks to spare.

Footnoting in this collection is essentially as original, meaning half-fledged Googlepedia hits for the first volume, standard scholarly footnoting in originally academic work, and naming of important sources in the remaining five out of seven volumes.

My apologies for readers who want footnotes; I know it's considered a sign of a serious or formal book, but I would rather make this collection available soon than wait indefinitely for all the half-fledged Googlepedia footnotes to be available.

Introduction

A scholar's dissertation may be a way to get to know him, and I present three roughly master's level dissertations (an applied math M.S. dissertation that was the first to take advantage of UIUC's newly available dissertation thesis option as well as the "Computational Science and Engineering" option that essentially made a math/computer science master's), a diploma dissertation in Biblical studies at Cambridge that my advisor described as "M.Phil. level work done to M.Phil. standards," and a master's dissertation from my next year's study.

They each offer a glimpse that may shed light on my "religion and science," or more precisely "technology and ascesis," orientation as a writer.

I do not specifically suggest that a humanities reader try to grok a thesis in pure math, but I suggest that readers with enough of an edge in mathematics, engineering, science, and technology might find it interesting and representing an unusual approach. The ordinary expectation that one might have of a dissertation in math is that it proves a theorem. This thesis does contain very minor theorems, but what it offers as significance is a structure in point-set topology, in between a topology or a metric space, that is similar to a metric space but you can't necessarily assign a real number to values in its metric. This in turn allows kinds of metric values that a standard metric space could not have, including a surprisingly easy rigorous way of handling infinitesimals such as great minds spent ages of trying to "exorcise" from differentiation in calculus. All of this may be taken as a curiosity and perhaps skipped for much of my intended audience, but it may be relevant to "religion and science" audiences to take this as a cue that I tried hard to obtain proficiency in mathematics, and tried to make suggestions that a mathematician might find interesting. There was no expectation for a master's thesis that it necessarily contributes something original, but it did then establish a small area which I then knew more about than anyone else in the world. Madly enough, my advisor and the other reader read about half and accepted it on the basis of the first half they had read.

My diploma thesis, in theology, takes a concept of "pattern" (traditionally described in opaquely colorless language as "a context, a set of forces in that context, and a resolution to those forces"), originally formulated in architecture and taken up by object-oriented computer programmers, and looks at cultural forces not in the Biblical text but cultural forces in Western, historical-critical scholarship of Biblical texts. Given what I said when I informally wrote up more or less what I wanted to do in a PhD thesis in theology, in " 'Religion and Science' Is Not Just Intelligent Design vs. Evolution," this may be surprising as I say somewhat nasty things about trying to mediate prestige to one's discipline by importing "a term from science." It was written shortly before I was received into the Orthodox Church, but I do not want to take the way out of saying "I was not Orthodox then and I would not repeat the line of argument." I would repeat the line of argument still. The explanation is that I was not trying to pull something from the prestige of science I had not studied, but drawing on my professional reading. The point in any case was not to mediate prestige, but drawing on what I considered and still consider a useful concept for what I analyzed. And to those who share this concern, I did not absolutely say in related conversation, "Do not draw on science in writing theology." I said to acquire a proficiency in science first, meaning "letters after your name," a suggestion that did not meet any warmth. I would comment further that although I have taken some physics classes, I do not draw on physics knowledge in that dissertation, and for that matter do not really draw on knowledge of physics at all outside of debunking what the rumor mill makes of e.g. the theory of relativity. I also critique and never endorse the Physics Envy Declaration, which declares that practitioners of one's humanity discipline are-scientists-and-they-are-just-as-much-scientists-as-people-in-the-so-called-"hard-sciences"-like-physics.

My second master's thesis, in theology, engages an area from the sciences (artificial intelligence), but instead of building on that to provide a tool to use in theology, but instead offering a theological critique that used theology to see things that are not seen in mainstream artificial intelligence research and for that matter are not seen in mainstream academic critiques of artificial intelligence. The attempt I make, whether or not it is deemed successful, is to add something besides a rubber stamp to the standard scientific enterprise. In " 'Religion and Science' Is Not Just Intelligent Design vs. Evolution," I suggest that academic theology take a cue from pop psychology, and more than that *bad* pop psychology, which in its discussion of boundaries is all about how you can only meaningfully say "Yes," when you have made a practice of saying "No," when you should say "No." This thesis, along those lines, is intended to offer an intelligent "No; I disagree with you and here's why," to a topic in the sciences where gullibility reigns.

The three dissertations represent something in relation to how I approach religion and science. The first is to know the science well if you are going to try to write about religion and science. To quote " 'Religion and Science' Is Not Just Intelligent Design vs. Evolution:"

> There is a sort of *Karate Kid* observation—"Karate is like a road. Know karate, safe. Don't know karate, safe. In the middle, *squash*, like a grape!"—that is relevant to theology and science. It has to do with, among other things, Gödel's Incompleteness Theorem, the question of evolution, and the like (perhaps I should mention the second law of thermodynamics). My point in this is not that there is an obligation to "know karate", that theologians need to earn degrees in the sciences before they are qualified to work as theologians, but that there is something perfectly respectable about "don't know karate."

And perhaps it helps to have just one blackbelt to say, "Don't know karate, safe," and argue against the inferiority complex that needs the Physics Envy Declaration.

My second dissertation shows a willingness to draw on science when it actually makes sense to do so. There is an endemic claim to introduce "a term from science," and "a term from science" is almost always used incorrectly, for the purpose of mediating prestige. My use of the concept of "pattern" in computer science is one that a programmer might recognize as a use outside of object-oriented computer programming, but perhaps also see as a successful transplant from computer science after object-oriented computer programmers transplanted the concept from its original articulation in architecture.

Finally, my third dissertation is an early work in exploring what theology can add to religion-science dialogue besides a rubber stamp: it sees things, on a humanities level, that the science practitioners do not see. One example is the "optimality assumption," which says or rather assumes that given the difficulties so far acknowledged by an artificial intelligence practitioner, artificial intelligence is optimally easy, so Turing apparently thought that if you gave conversation asking for a poetry sample to be composed, a chess problem to be answered, and two numbers to be added, extracting these "real" problems from free-form English would come along more or less for free. (History has not been kind to appearances of the "optimality assumption.") I leave in my treatment of the occult, but I felt defiled when doing my research, and there are some sins it is best to know as little about as possible. Possibly my treatment of the occult is enticing, but that is a fault and not to my credit as a writer. (Someone better might show the banality of evil.)

These represent stepping stones along the way to my interest in theology and faith. Please note that none of these three dissertations really gets into the core question that motivates this collection as a whole, namely how to best engage (and refrain from engaging) with technology to best support Orthodox ascesis. None of the dissertations broach the question of whether or how a mainstream technology use is helpful for the spiritual condition of the person using it. The material I wanted to use for a Ph.D. thesis, as given non-scholarly write-up in " 'Religion and Science' Is Not Just Intelligent Design vs. Evolution," does not yet see the fruitfulness of this question either. It approaches this territory more directly than even my third dissertation, which starts to say things that are non-redundant to science, for instance the endemic import of "a term from science," but does not articulate, as I later would in "A Guide to Technology's Hidden Price Tags:"

> As I discussed in " 'Religion And Science' Is Not Just Intelligent Design Vs. Evolution," one of the forms of name-dropping in academic theology is to misuse "a term from science": the claim to represent "a term from science" is endemic in academic theology, but I can count on the fingers of one hand the number of times I've read "a term from science" that was used correctly.
>
> One book said it was going to introduce "a term from computer science," *toggling*, which meant switching rapidly between several applications. The moral of this story was that we should

switch rapidly between multiple activities in our daily lives.

What I would have said earlier is, "While that moral might be true, what it is not is a lesson from computer science." What I would say now is, "Never mind if that is a lesson from computer science. The moral is fundamentally flawed."

I don't know exactly how useful or useless my theology dissertations will be to the reader. It is not a compliment to say that an author's tone is academic, although scholars have complained that my tone is not academic enough, reading like opinion pieces. (I was formed as a writer by reading C.S. Lewis, and my work has an apologetic bent.) I also don't find any of these three dissertations to representing my most interesting work or my main contribution as a writer. It is this series as a whole that represents my magnum opus; these dissertations may serve to some readers as three chapters of an intellectual autobiography. It is offered in a spirit of laying cards out on the table, for the reader who is curious about insights into my formation.

Introduction to "Closeness Spaces: An Elementary Exploration of Generalized Metric Spaces, and Ordered Fields Derived from Them"

This represents a significant phase of the author's early career. It may be inaccessible to most readers, but even knowing it is there may help the reader understand how the author grew up in the heart of mathematics, engineering, technology, and science, and from that point came to repenting further of unhelpful use of technology.

The author's first masters was an applied math degree so as to have the computational science and engineering option, but is a dissertation in pure math.

Closeness Spaces: Elementary Explorations Into Generalized Metric Spaces, and Ordered Fields Derived From Them

University of Illinois at Urbana-Champaign
Department of Mathematics
Closeness Spaces:
Elementary Explorations Into Generalized Metric Spaces,
and Ordered Fields Derived From Them

Jonathan Hayward
Master's Thesis
Advisor: John Gray
May 6, 1998

Abstract

A generalization of metric spaces is examined, in which we are able to determine which of two pairs of points is closer (or if both are equally close), but not initially know how to assign a number to a distance. After the spaces are defined in general, we look at some more specific closeness spaces, and establish the existence of a metric, which we are able to determine, under certain broad circumstances.

After looking at the closeness spaces, more specific attention is devoted to the closenesses themselves. We begin to define arithmetic operations over closeness spaces, and (given certain restrictions on the space) then complete addition and subtraction to develop a totally ordered group in which the closenesses are embedded. We prove that it is indeed a totally ordered field, and look at some examples. Directions are suggested for future research.

[Side note when entering this dissertation two decades later: this research includes a way to rigorously define and use infinitesimals. Infinitesimals were long seen as something you wanted to have but could not rigorously define; epsilon-delta proofs in relation to derivatives in calculus represent a masterstroke of how to do an infinitesimal's job using only standard real numbers for epsilons and deltas. Infinitesimals were spoken of as a ghost to be exorcized, and the entire point epsilon-delta proofs were a way to circumvent obvious use of infinitesimals in a mathematically rigorous way. At the time this thesis was written there appear to have been rigorous treatment of infinitesimals; however, so far as one could tell this approach to providing this kind of squeaky-clean rigorous handling of infinitesimals was new when the thesis was written.]

Introduction

Intuitively, a closeness space is like a metric space, with balls, symmetry, positive definiteness, and a triangle inequality, boundaries, an induced topology, and other familiar attributes of a metric space. However, it is a space for which we do not specifically know a metric: it is possible that we simply do not know a metric or none is given, or that no metric may exist. The latter holds in certain cases where the real numbers are too coarse of an ordered field to describe the space's distances: such a thing is possible, for instance, when there are infinitesimal and infinite distances. A closeness space might not be thought of so much as a generalization of a metric space (at least in the sense that a metric space is a generalization of $\mathbb{R}n$), but rather as a metric space with a generalization of real-valued distances. It is a metric space which may potentially have nonstandard real numbers (broadly defined) as its distances, rather than necessarily having real numbers under the standard model as its distances.]

In this sense, what is of interest is not only the spaces themselves, but their distances: what kind of group embeds them (we will look at a field which embeds an arithmetic closure of these distances). We will study the topological spaces, but our interest is not only in the spaces, but in the ordered groups and then fields which embed the closenesses. Throughout this thesis, the aim is both to establish certain elementary properties — laying a groundwork — and also to suggest directions for future research.

It is remarked that the approach is not to start with a field and then see for what kind of spaces it can function like a metric; the approach is rather to start with a space and see what kind of field acts as an arithmetic closure to its closenesses, given a certain construction.

Chapter 1: Notation, Definitions and Terminology
Notation 1:1:

In this document, a lowercase, indexed variable name is generally understood to be an element of the set designated by the corresponding uppercase letter, provided that the letter is 's' or occurs after 's' in the alphabet. For example:

s1 ∈ S

      Furthermore, we associate in the same way α with indexing set J, and β with K. These indexing sets are understood to have no last element.
      There will be plainly marked exceptions to this rule.

Definition 1:2:

      A closeness space C is a set S, together with a function

$$f: S \times S \times S \times S \mapsto \{\text{'<'}, \text{'='}, \text{'>'}\}$$

such that the following conditions hold:

Definition 1.2.1:

      f is defined for each quadruplet of points in S.
      (S is said to be a space, and its elements are referred to as its points, as elsewhere in topology. The function f is said to be a closeness.)
      Intuitively, this condition and those following guarantee that f is comparing the distance between the first two points, and the distance between the last two points to see which one is greater. This condition, and the next four, are simply conditions which guarantee that f is well-behaved as a function on a pair of pairs of points, only depends on which pair of pairs of points is given, and defines a total ordering up to equivalence classes.
      For every six points s1, s2, s3, s4, s5, and s6 (possibly non-distinct), we have the following conditions hold:

C.J.S. Hayward

Condition 1.2.2:

$f(s_1, s_2, s_3, s_4) = f(s_2, s_1, s_3, s_4)$
$f(s_1, s_2, s_3, s_4) = f(s_3, s_4, 11, s_3)$

f is not affected by swapping the elements in one pair, or by swapping the pairs. This is the closeness space's version of a metric space requiring symmetry.

Condition 1.2.3:

If $f(s_1, s_2, s_3, s_4) = \text{`<'}$, then $f(s_3, s_4, s_1, s_2) = \text{`>'}$.
If $f(s_1, s_2, s_3, s_4) = \text{`='}$, then $f(s_3, s_4, s_1, s_2) = \text{`='}$.
If $f(s_1, s_2, s_3, s_4) = \text{`>'}$, then $f(s_3, s_4, s_1, s_2) = \text{`<'}$.

Condition 1.2.4:

If $f(s_1, s_2, s_3, s_4) = \text{`<'}$ and $f(s_3, s_4, s_5, s_6) = \text{`<'}$, then $f(s_1, s_2, s_5, s_6) = \text{`<'}$.

Condition 1.2.5:

We have

$f(s_1, s_2, s_1, s_2) = \text{`='}$

Condition 1.2.6:

If s_2 and s_3 are distinct, then we have

$f(s_1, s_1, s_2, s_3) = \text{`<'}$

Every point is closer to itself than the distance between any pair of distinct points; this is the closeness space's version of the positive definiteness of a metric space.

Condition 1.2.7:

We have

$$f(s1, s1, s2, s2) = \text{'='}$$

In other words, there is only one zero. It may be mathematically interesting to remove this restriction, but we will not investigate that possibility.

Condition 1.2.8:

If $f(s1, s3, s1, s2) = \text{'<'}$ then for every set $T \subset S$ containing points arbitrarily close to s3 (in a sense to be defined below), there exists t1 ≠ s3, such that, for every point s4, if $f(s3, s4, s1, s2) = \text{'<'}$.
(What this is getting at, is that if you have a boundary point s2 to a ball (boundary being outside the ball as with metric spaces), then every point closer to the center than the boundary point has a neighborhood entirely contained inside the ball (closer to the center than the boundary point). This means that a ball with a boundary point has a unique radius: there cannot be a second boundary point further than the center than the first boundary point, because then the first boundary point would be inside the ball; there also cannot be a secondary point closer to the center than the first boundary point, because this axiom says that every closer point has a neighborhood.)

Condition 1.2.9:

A set $T \subset S$ is said to hold points arbitrarily close to point s3 (in a sense to be defined below), there exists t1 ≠ s3, such that if $f(s2, t1, s2, s4) = \text{'<'}$, then $f(s1, s4, s1, s2) = \text{'>'}$.

(Here, we say that if you have a boundary point s2 to a ball, then every point further from the center than the boundary point has a neighborhood disjoint from the ball. Note that these two conditions may be vacuously satisfied by finite or other discrete metric / closeness spaces, with which we are not very much concerned.)

These two stipulations together constitute the closeness space's version of the triangle inequality in a metric space. The slight awkwardness of this definition is necessary to permit discrete metric spaces. This awkwardness will recur in other places where we are defining concepts on a very low level without using familiar tools (because we are developing a more general form of such tools), but it should pass.

Definition 1:3:

A set $T \subset S$ is said to contain points arbitrarily close to point s1 if the following conditions hold:

Condition 1.3.1:

T is nonempty and contains at least one point distinct from s1.

Condition 1.3.2:

For every distinct pair of points s2 and s3, there exists T1 distinct from s1 so that $f(s1, t1, s2, s3) = \text{'<'}$.

(In other words, for every closeness in the space, there is a point in T that is closer to s1.)

Additional terminology 1.4:

Term 1.4.1:

Point s1 is said to be closer to s2 than s3 is (close to s2) when $f(s2, t1, s2, s4) = \text{'<'}$.

Term 1.4.2:

Points s1 and r are said to be equidistant from s2 when $f(s1, s2, r, s2) = \text{'='}$.

Term 1.4.3:

Point s1 is said to be father from s2 than r is when $f(s1, s2, r, s2) = \text{'>'}$.

Term 1.4.4:

A pair of points is referred to as a distance.

Term 1.4.5:

The pair (s1, s2) is said to be the distance from s1 to s2.

Condition 1.4.6:

If distance d1 is the pair (s1, s2) and distance d2 is the pair (s3, s4), then the following three conditions hold:

Condition 1.4.6.1:

If $f(s1, s2, s3, s4) = \text{'<'}$, then d1 is said to be less than d2, written d1 < d2.

Condition 1.4.6.2:

If $f(s_1, s_2, s_3, s_4)$ = '=', then d_1 is said to be equal to d_2, written $d_1 = d_2$.

Condition 1.4.6.3:

If $f(s_1, s_2, s_3, s_4)$ = '>', then d_1 is said to be greater than d_2, written $d_1 > d_2$.

Remark 1:5:

Equality induces a partition of equivalence on distance. We will abuse notation slightly by referring to a distance, its equivalence class, and elements of its equivalence class interchangeably. Context should make clear which of these is meant; if context is not sufficient to clarify, then we will be more explicit as to which of these is intended.

Definition 1.6:

A ball about point s_1 is a set of points such that the following two conditions hold:

Condition 1.6.1:

Every point in the ball is closer to s_1 than is every point not in the ball.

Condition 1.6.2:

There does not exist point s_2 in the ball such that the following conditions hold:

Condition 1.6.2.1:

No point in the ball is further from s_1 than s_2 is.

Condition 1.6.2.2:

S contains points arbitrarily lose to s2, which are not contained in B.

This latter condition guarantees that B does not contain its boundary, if it does have a nonempty boundary.

As the remainder of the definition and terminology, we have:

Condition 1.6.3:

If distance d = (s1, r), r is not contained in B, and B contains points arbitrarily close to r, then ball B is said to of radius d, or to be the ball of radius d centered at p, and its boundary is said to be the circle of radius d centered at p.

(By the remarks following the triangle inequality, there is at most one equivalence class of distances which satisfy this property. Note that a ball might or might not necessarily have a radius.)

Definition 1.7:

A set T is said to have points arbitrarily close to point s1 if T contains at least one point t1 ≠ s1, and for every t2 ≠ s1, there exists t3 which is closer to s1 than is t2.

Definition 1.8:

The boundary of a set T is the set U of points u such that both T contains points arbitrarily close to u, and S\T contain points arbitrarily close to u.

Definition of values, having different levels, 1.9:

We are using the term value to refer to mathematical objects which we will use in the construction of the field we are working on. Each value has a level; values of higher levels are determined in terms of values of lower level. The highest level of value will be an element of a field. I will define some (not all) levels of values here. If we use the term without specifying its level, it should be understood to be the last level specified, usually the highest level so far defined, if there is ambiguity. In some cases we will leave an ambiguity when what we are saying applies both to a member of an equivalence class, and its class.

Definition 1.9.1:

A level 0 value is defined to be a distance (strictly defined as a pair of points).

Definition 1.9.2:

A level 1 value is defined to be an equivalence class of level 0 values under the partition induced by equality. Level 1 values are ordered, in the same way that their members are ordered.

The remaining levels of values will be defined after I have begun to build up the machinery necessary to explain and use them.

Definition 1.10:

A level 0 zero is defined to be a distance (s1, s1).

Definition 1.11:

A level 1 zero is defined to be the equivalence class of level 0 zeroes. Zeroes will be defined for all levels greater than or equal to level a.

Definition 1.12:

A level n value is defined to be positive if it is greater than the level n zero.

Definition 1.13:

A level n sequence is defined to be a level n sequence $\{\in_\alpha\}\alpha\in J$, with J a totally ordered indexing set.

A level n epsilon is defined to be a level n sequence $\{\in_\alpha\}\alpha\in J$, of positive level n values, such that the following two conditions hold:

Condition 1.13.1:

Every positive level n value v is greater than some $\varepsilon\alpha$.

Condition 1.13.2:

Every $\varepsilon\alpha$ is greater than or equal to every $\varepsilon\beta$.

Definition 1.13.3:

Distance d_1 is said to be within distance d_2 of distance d_3 if there is a set of points s_1, s_2, and s_3 such that $d_1 = (s_1, s_2)$, $d_2 \leq (s_3)$, and $d_3 = (s_1, ss_3)$.

Chapter 2: Examples

Example 2.1:

Every metric space is a closeness space. Two distances are compared by '<'.

Example 2.2:

We derive a space C from ℝ2 under the Euclidean metric as follows:

We make C a copy of ℝ2, and then we add a point O' to the space, and define closenesses as follows:

O' is as close to every non-origin point as the origin is.

O' and the origin are closer than any other distinct pair of points.

Theorem 2.2.1:

This closeness space cannot be described by any metric.

Proof:

We prove this by contradiction.

Assume that such a metric exists.

If a metric did induce this closeness, it would have a least nonzero distance d, the distance from the origin O to O'.

Let the distance from O to (0, 1) be d'.

By the Archimedean property, there exists n such that $d' \div n < d$.

By repeated application of the triangle inequality on segments from (0, 0) to $(i \div n, 0)$ and from $(i \div n, 0)$ to $((i + 1) \div n, 0)$, this means that d' is at most equal to n times the distance from (0, 0) to $(1 \div n, 0)$.

This means that the distance from (0, 0) to $(1 \div n, 0)$ is less than d, but it is positive because they are two distinct points, and d is a minimal positive distance. ⇒⇐

Q.E.D.

This space is in many ways a space very like a metric space; although it boasts unusual decoration, it has a strong amount of structure, like a metric space, structure that might not be present in an arbitrary metric space.

Example 2.3:

Let M be a metric space with metric μ over a set E of equivalence classes partitioning a set S. Then we can define a closeness space C which has S as its space, and its closeness f defined as follows:
For every four points s1, s2, s3, s4 in S:

Case 2.3.1:

If $\mu(s1, s2) < \mu(s3, s4)$, then $f(s1, s2, s3, s4) =$ '<'.

Case 2.3.2:

If $\mu(s1, s2) > \mu(s3, s4)$, then $f(s1, s2, s3, s4) =$ '>'.

Case 2.3.3:

If $\mu(s1, s2) = \mu(s3, s4)$, then:

Case 2.3.3.1

If s1 = s2 and s3 = s4 then $f(s1, s2, s3, s4) =$ '='.

Case 2.3.3.2

If s1 ≠ s2 and s3 = s4 then $f(s1, s2, s3, s4) =$ '>'.

Case 2.3.3.3

If s1 = s2 and s3 ≠ s4 then f(s1, s2, s3, s4) = '<'.

Case 2.3.3.4

If s1 ≠ s2 and s3 ≠ s4 then f(s1, s2, s3, s4) = '='.

In other words, if we have a metric space over equivalence classes, we can compare distances between pairs of elements of the classes by first looking at the distance between the elements' equivalence classes, and then doing something else to break ties — say, seeing where they are the same.

In relation to this, we have:

Definition and example 2.4:

If we have two closeness spaces C and D, with underlying sets S and T, then we can take their cross product E = C × D, with underlying sets S and T, then we can take their product E = C × D, with closenesses compared in the dictionary order.

Specifically, let U be the underlying set for E. We compare two distances d1 = (u1, u2) and d2 = (u3, u4), with u1 = (s1, t1) and d2 = (u2, u2), u3 = (s3, s3), and u4 = (s4, t4), as follows:

Case 2.4.1:

If (s1, s2) < (s3, s4), then (u1, u2) < (u3, u4).

Case 2.4.2:

If (s1, s2) > (s3, s4), then (u1, u2) > (u3, u4).

Case 2.4.3:

If (s1, s2) = (s3, s4), then:

Case 2.4.3.1:

If (t1, t2) > (t3, t4), then (u1, u2) > (t3, t4).

Case 2.4.3.2:

If (t1, t2) < (t3, t4), then (u1, u2) < (t3, t4).

Case 2.4.3.3:

If (t1, t2) = (t3, t4), then (u1, u2) = (t3, t4).

N.B. This cross product, in the dictionary order, will be used later.

Example 2.4.4:

Let S, T = $\mathbb{R}2$ under the closeness induced by the Euclidean metric. Then U = S $\times$ T may be described as a Euclidean plane, where each point is itself identified with a miniature Euclidean plane. It is a plane with infinitesimal distances, or alternately an infinitesimal Euclidean plane.
A typical ball in this space is the ball with center at the origin ((0, 0), (0, 0)) consisting of all points strictly closer to the origin than ((1, 1), (1, 1)). This divides the large-scale plane into three regions: the interior, exterior, and boundary of the disk of radius 1, centered at the origin. The interior of the disk corresponds to miniature planes which are entirely within the ball, where every point is inside. The exterior of the disk corresponds to miniature planes which are entirely outside the ball, where no point is inside. The boundary of the disk corresponds to miniature planes where the interior of the disk of radius 1 centered at the origin (of

the small one, not the large plane or metric space) is inside the ball, and its boundary and exterior are outside. The boundary of the given ball in U consists of, in the miniature planes, all circles of radius 1 centered at the origin which are themselves on the circle of radius 1 in the large plane.

Proof that this satisfies the axioms of the space:

The set of equivalence classes (under equality) of closenesses has a 1-1 order-preserving mapping to the nonnegative real number line cross itself, in the dictionary order. In other words, it is a dictionary order cross product of two totally ordered sets, and therefore totally orders. This satisfies axioms 1.2.1-1.2.7.

To satisfy 1.2.8, we let s2 be closer to s3 than is s3.

If the small planes of s2 and s3 are equidistant to the small plane of s1, then the small plane position of s2 is closer to the small plane position of s1 than is the small plane position of s3. There is, by topology, an open disk about the small plane position of s1 and boundary the small plane position of s3; if we take such a disk in the small plane s3 is actually contained in, it has points arbitrarily close to s3, and is contained in the disk of center s1 and boundary s2.

Every set T containing points arbitrarily close to s3 intersects the aforementioned disk infinitely many times. So we take some point inside that as our t1; every point s4 closer to s3 than is t1 and therefore closer to s1 than is s2.

The same argument holds in the case that the small plane of s3 is closer to the small plane of s1 than is the small plane of s2, save that we simply choose any disk contained in the small plane of s3.

1.2.9 is satisfied; we simply have an open disk outside the open disk of center s1 and boundary point s2 instead of inside.

Remark 2.4.4.1

Note that in this case, a ball in the cross product was not a cross product of two balls, but the boundary of a ball in the cross product was cross product of the boundary of two balls. This leads us to:

Theorem 2.4.4.2:

Let C and D be closeness spaces with underlying sets S and T, both of which consist of more than one point. Let space $E = C \times D$, with underlying set $U = S \times T$. Let ball B be a ball in E which does not contain any points (s_2, t_2) for any point s_2 and some point t_2, contains all points (s_3, t_3) for any point t and some point t_3, and is centered at point $u_1 = (s_1, t_1)$.

Then B is not the cross product of two balls, but the boundary of B is the cross product of the boundaries of two balls. Furthermore, if the aforementioned boundray is nonempty and contains point $u_4 = (s_4, t_4)$, then the boundary consists of the cross product of the circle of radius (s_1, s_4) of radius (t_1, t_4) centered at t_1.

N.B. All of the hypotheses, which informally could be described as looking like clutter, are needed only to rule out degenerate exceptions. There are a number of equivalent replacements for the requirement that B contains no points at one T coordinate and all points at another.

Proof:

Proof by contradiction that B is not the cross product of two balls:

Assume that B is the cross product of two balls. B contains all of the points at one T coordinate, t_3, and none at another, t_2. Therefore, B contains $u_5 = (s_5, t_5$ with $s_5 \neq$

s1. Every point (s1, t6) is closer to u1 than is u5, so B contains a point at T coordinate t, and also does not contain that point. ⇒⇐

Q.E.D.

We consider two cases now:

Case 2.4.4.2.1:

B has an empty boundary. In that case, the further claim is vacuously true because the 'if' clause is not met. In addition, the former claim is also at least vacuously true: we observe that an entire space constitutes a ball, and the boundary of the entire space is empty. Therefore we examine the more interesting

Case 2.4.4.2.2:

B has a nonempty boundary. In that case, we observe that all points on the boundary are equidistant from some point u1; if one were closer to another, we would have an exception to the triangle inequality.

I claim that if (s7, t7) and (s8, t8) are in the boundary B, then so are (s7, t8) and (s8, t7):

Assume that (s7, t7) and (ss8, t8 are in the boundary B. Then we can say the following, both for sets of points contained in B, and sets of points disjoint from B: there exists a set U7 ⊂ U containing points arbitrarily close to (s7, t7), and a set U8 ⊂ U containing points (s8, t8). U7 is a set of ordered pairs of points, which contain points of arbitrary close S coordinate to s7, and a set U8 ⊂ U containing points arbitrarily close to (s8, t8). U7 is a set of ordered pairs of points, which contains points of arbitrarily close S coordinate to s7, and arbitrarily close T coordinate to t7, and U8 is a set of ordered pairs of points, which contains points of arbitrarily close S coordinate to s8, and arbitrarily close T coordinate to t8. Take the cross product V of the S coordinates in U7 and the T coordinates contained in U8, and the cross product W of the S coordinates contained in U8, and the T coordinates contained in U7. As this argument applies both to sets of points contained in B, and sets of points disjoint from B, we have (s7, t8) and (s8, t8) as desired.

This establishes the independence of the S and T coordinates of points on the boundary, so the boundary is a cross product of some pair of sets in S and T.

These sets must be equidistant from s1 and t1 respectively; if they were not, then we could select two radii of different length for the ball, and violate the triangle inequality. So they are subsets of the boundaries of balls; they must be the whole boundary because the cross product of two accumulation points of different sets is an accumulation point of the cross product of the two sets, as we argued above. And this establishes that the radius of the boundary must be the distance from the center to the cross product of two respective boundary points. So we have the boundary of B, for u4 = (s1, s4) a point on the boundary, equal to the cross product of the circles of radius (s1, s4) and (t1, t4) centered at s1 and t1 respectively, as desired.

Q.E.D.

Example 2.5:

Any subset of a closeness space is a closeness space.

Remark 2.6:

The operations of taking a cross product of two closeness spaces in the dictionary order, and taking a subset of a closeness space, are together quite powerful. All other examples here are special cases of the operations taking a cross product of two closeness spaces in the dictionary order, and taking the subset of a closeness space.

Example 2.6.1:

The disjoint union of two closeness spaces C and D, in other words a union where C and D retain their closeness functions, and every function in one space is closer than every function in another space, is achievable by taking $\mathbb{R} \times$ C, paring it down until we have only a copy of (0, 1) where 0 is identified with a copy of C, and then taking the cross product of the result in D, and again paring it down until we only have a copy of (0, 1)where 0 is identified with a copy of C for which each element is identified with a single element, and 1 is identified with a copy of D.

If we allow not only finite but transfinite sequences of these two operations (which must be well-ordered, in order to be well-defined), then possible closeness spaces can take an almost unbelievable complexity beyond what is possible for metric spaces. The faintest hint of this is provided by a transfinite algorithm, and partial proof of correctness which is not reproduced here, which seems (given the Axiom of Choice) to be able to embed an arbitrary partial ordering in a totally ordered field. I believe that the power is sufficient to justify making:

Conjecture 2.6.2:

Assuming the Axiom of Choice, any closeness space can be generated from $\mathbb{R}$ under the closeness arising from the usual Euclidean distance metric, by the operation of taking cross products in the dictionary order, and taking subsets.

Example 2.7:

The long line appears to be a closeness space under what could intuitively be described as comparing the absolute value of differences. In general we cannot subtract ordinals as we can finite numbers, but we can do something comparable in this case.

We compare pairs of ordinals (o1, o2) and (o3, o4) as follows, in the case that both are distinct pairs:

Without loss of generality, assume that o1 < o2 and o3 < o4.

f(o1, o2, o3, o4) = '<' if o1 + o4 < o3 + o2.

f(o1, o2, o3, o4) = '=' if o1 + o4 = o3 + o2.

f(o1, o2, o3, o4) = '>' if o1 + o4 > o3 + o2.

Example 2.8:

The numbering of items in this thesis may be taken to be a finite and discrete closeness space, with closeness compared with a dictionary ordering on the numberings.

Chapter 3: Towards Constructing a Field

We now define the next level of values:

Definition 3.1:

A level 2 value is defined to be a level 1 sequences of values {dα}$\alpha \in$J which is Cauchy convergent: for every element $\epsilon\beta$ of level 1 epsilon {eβ}$\beta \in$K, there exists an element dβ of {dα such that every subsequent pair of values dα1, dα2 are within $\epsilon\beta$ of each other.

What we are doing here is taking the closure of the set of level 1 values under the operation of taking limits, which might or might not be embeddable in $\mathbb{R}$ and might be finer-grained. A level 1 value is included by a sequence that consists exclusively of that value.

Note 3.2:

We compare two level 2 values $v1 = \{d1\alpha\}\alpha{\in}J$ and $v2 = \{d2\alpha\}\alpha{\in}J$ as follows:

If there is an element $\alpha0$ of J such that, for all subsequent values of $\alpha1$ and $\alpha2$ we have $\alpha1$ and $\alpha2$ then $v1 \leq v2$.

If there is an element $\alpha0$ of J such that, for all subsequent values of $\alpha1$ and $\alpha2$ we have $\alpha1$ and $\alpha2$ then $v1 \geq v2$.

If for every element $\alpha0$ of J, there exist subsequent $\alpha1$, $\alpha2$, $\alpha3$, and $\alpha4$ such that $d1\alpha1 \leq d2\alpha2$ and $d1\alpha3 \leq d2\alpha4$, then $v1 = v2$.

Definition 3.3:

A level 3 value is defined to be an equivalence class of level 2 values under the partition induced by equality. Level 3 values are ordered in the same way that their members are ordered.

Definition 3.4:

A level 2 zero is defined to be an infinite sequence of level 1 zeroes.

Definition 3.5:

The level 3 zero is defined to be the equivalence class of the level 2 zeroes.

Lemma 3.6:

The set of points whose distances are less than v1 from point s1, for any value v1 and point s1, constitutes a ball.

Proof:

It is clear that every point in this set is closer to s1 than is any point not in the set. So we need only to know that the set does not contain any boundary points.

If there is a boundary point s2, then there is an epsilon at that boundary point contained in the set, and an epsilon at that boundary disjoint from the set. From these can be chosen a sequence of distances that converges to (s1, s2) and is inside the set, whereby $v1 \geq (s1, s2)$, and can also b chosen by a sequence of distances that converges to (s1, s2) and is outside the set, whereby $v1 \leq (s1, s2)$. So $v1 = (s1, s2)$. The ball contains only points strictly closer than v1, so it does not contain s2. $\Rightarrow\Leftarrow$

Q.E.D.

Definition 3.7:

The supremum (resp. infemum) of a nonempty set W of level 2 values is defined to be the equivalence class containing the sequences v1 of values which satisfy the following three conditions:

Condition 3.7.1:

All elements of v1 are contained in some element of W.

Condition 3.7.2:

v1 contains at least one element greater than (resp. less than) or equal to any element of W.

Condition 3.7.3:

$v1$ is monotonically nondecreasing (resp. nonincreasing).

Remark 3.7.4:

Not all sets will necessarily have a supremum or infemum. This a definition of what the supremum is if it exists, not necessarily a statement that one always exists.

There is at most a single equivalence class containing all such sequences, because any one contains an element greater than or equal to any element of any other, arbitrarily far along in the sequence.

The supremum and infemum of the empty set are undefined.

Now, we begin to develop an arithmetic.

Definition 3.8:

A value $v1$ is said to be equal to $v2 + v3$ if $v1$ is the supremum over all triplets of points $s1$, $s2$, and $s3$ of the distance $(s1, s3)$, such that the following two conditions hold:

Condition 3.8.1:

$(s1, s2) \leq v2$
$(s2, s3)\ v3$

Condition 3.8.2:

There do not exist any three points $s4$, $s5$, and $s6$ such that:

$(s4, s4) \leq v2$
$(s5, s6) < v3$
$(s4, s6) \geq v1$

or

$(s4, s4) < v2$
$(s5, s6) \leq v2$
$(s4, s6) \geq v1$

Notation 3.8.3:

A value v1 is said to be a difference of v2 and v3 if v2 = sub1 + v3.

Remark 3.8.4:

This definition does not guarantee the existence of a sum of two values; it only tells how to tell if a given value is equal to the sum of two others.

This value is chosen for its simplicity, specificity, and power; there numerous other ways of defining addition, some of which would seem to be a more generalized version of addition, doing to addition in ordered, cyclic, abelian groups as we know them what metric spaces do to $\mathbb{R}2$. However, we will not investigate that generality here, and in particular, we are going to restrict our attention to a specific subset of closeness spaces, those for which addition as here defined is associative and uniquely defined.

If we not only do not restrict our attention, but replace the given condition with the stipulation that v1 is the supremum over points s1 of distances from s1 is the supremum over points s1 of distances from s1 to a point in the union of all closed balls of radius v3 whose centers lie in a closed ball of radius v2 centered at s1, then we further lose commutativity; at least in the case of the long line, though, we have reproduced ordinal addition.

It appears that looking at those more general cases may be of mathematical interest and may allow the creation of an arithmetic that is looser and more general than that of an ordered, abelian group. However, we do not investigate that possibility here, and have not investigated it, beyond the brief attention paid in this remark.

This definition provides commutativity, and unique subtraction where defined (i.e. $v_1 - v_2$ may not be defined, but if it is, it is unique; provided that $v_1 - v_2$ may not be defined, but if it is, it is unique; provided that $v_1 = v_2 + v_3$, if $v_4 < v_3$, then the distances between pairs of points eligible for the definition of addition will be less by at least a minimum positive amount, by the triangle inequality, so $v_2 + v_4 < v_2 + v_3 = v_1$. This observation, as well as establishing that subtraction is not ambiguous (though possibly undefined), proves for us:

Theorem 3.9:

For any three values v_1, v_2, and v_3 for which $v_2 +$ is defined, we have:

If $v_1 < v_2$, then $v_1 + v_3 < v_2 + v_3$.
If $v_1 = v_2$, then $v_1 + v_3 = v_2 + v_3$.
If $v_1 > v_2$, then $v_1 + v_3 > v_2 + v_3$.

Sketch of Proof 3.9.1:

The first case is established above. The second case is established from the first case by the symmetry of an ordering, and the third case is established by the contradiction which would arise from the transitivity of the ordering if one sum was less than the other.

We now define our next level of value; as we earlier developed a closure under the operation of taking limits, we now define a closure under the operation of addition. Again, we are going with the more specific and powerful definition of addition given, at the loss of some generality.

Hunch 3.10:

Addition of values is associative.

Suggestion of Proof Idea 3.10.1:

It seems that this arises from condition 3.8.2. Definition 3.8 is a refined version of earlier, less powerful definitions; we have not devoted enough time to the matter to establish associativity. We will continue on the assumption that this is true; one might say if need be that we are restricting our attention to spaces where addition is associative. We will further restrict attention to spaces which are closed under addition (although a slightly weaker condition is needed for my work, namely that any two level 4 values as defined below are uniquely comparable).

Definition 3.11:

A level 4 value is defined to be a finite string of symbols as follows:

Part 3.11.1:

If v1 is a variable referring to a level 3 value, then "v1" is a level 4 value.

Part 3.11.2:

If "s1" and "s2" are two level 4 values, then "(s1 + s2) is a level 4 value.

Part 3.11.3:

If "s1" is a level 4 value, then so is "— s1".

Part 3.11.4:

Nothing else is a level 4 value.
We compare level 4 values as follows:

Comparison 3.11.5:

If for level 3 values we have v1 < v2, then for level 4 values, we have "v1" < "v2" and "— v1" > " — v2".
If for level 3 values we have v1 = v2, then for level 4 values, we have "v1" = "v2" and "— v1" > " — v2".
If for level 3 values we have v1 > v2, then for level 4 values, we have "v1" > "v2" and "— v1" < " — v2".
And we complete comparison by allowing certain manipulations, namely:

Part 3.11.6:

If for level 3 values we have v1 = v2 + v3, then inside a level 4 value v1 may be substituted or back-substituted for v2 + v3 and v3 + v2, then inside a level 4 value v2 may be substituted or back-substituted for v1 + — v3.

Part 3.11.7:

We may associate and commute while preserving equality.

Part 3.11.8:

We may add a like value to two different values without affecting their comparison.

Part 3.11.9:

Comparison is transitive.

We now define:

Definition 3.12:

A level 5 value is an equivalence class of level 4 values under equality, with addition, additive inversion, and comparison of equivalence classes defined according to the equivalence classes of those operations on respective members.
We now have an ordered abelian group.

Remark 3.13:

It is well known that an ordered abelian group may be embedded in a field. (Source: Anand Pillay).

Definition 3.14:

For any two values v1 and v2, v1 is said to be of the same magnitude as v2 if there exists a positive natural number n such that either $v1 + v1 + \cdots + v1 > v2$ (with v1 added to itself nn times) and $v2 + v2 + v2 \cdots v2 > v1$ (with v2 added to itself n times), or $v1 + v1 + \cdots + v1 < -v2$ (with v1 added to itself nn times) and $-v2 - v2 - v2 \cdots - v2 < v1$ (with v2 added to itself n times).
It is clear that the magnitudes are equivalence classes of values.

The value 0 resides in its own magnitude, which will not be named.

Part 3.14.1:

Magnitude M1 is said to be greater than (resp. less than) magnitude M2 if it is a different magnitude, and M1 contains at least one positive value that is greater than (resp. less than) at least one positive value in M2.

Part 3.14.2:

The magnitude which contains 1 is said to be finite.

All greater magnitudes than the finite magnitude are said to be infinite.

All lesser magnitudes than the finite magnitude (excluding the magnitude of 0), are said to be infinitesimal. The variable ε will hereafter refer to an infinitesimal.

To give a specific example of what kind of ordered field we have, let us look at

Example 3.15:

Let closeness space C be the space examined in example 2.3.4, namely $R2 \times R2$, under the closenesses induced by the dictionary order on Euclidean closenesses.

Then the closenesses are of type $R2 \times R2$, in the dictionary order.

The elements of a minimal imbedding field are of order type $S \subset R2Z$, such that all but finitely many of the coordinates of an element of S are zero.

Comparison of values is a dictionary comparison of their coordinates.

Addition of two values is coordinate-wise addition of reals. I.e. if v1 and v2 are values and v1i, v2i are the ith coordinates of v_1 and v_2 respectively, then the ith coordinate of v_{3i} of $v_3 = v_1 + v_2$ is equal to $v_{1i} + v_{2i}$.

Multiplication of two values is as follows:

If v_1 and v_1 are as above, then v_3 has coordinate v_{3i} equal to $\Sigma_{j+k=i} = v_{1j} \times v_{2k}$.

This is isomorphic to the field of ratios of polynomials in a single variable, over the real numbers. Note that, although the order type is fixed, a constant c chosen so that $c_0 = 1$, c_1 is a number of the lowest infinite magnitude and zero coordinate in other magnitudes, and c_{-1} is a number of the highest infinitesimal magnitudes, is not a unique constant. Any one such value can be arrived at by multiplying another such value by a nonzero real number.

The interpretation of this representation as given is that the 0-coordinate is the finite component, components of positive $\mathbb{Z}$ value are infinite components, and components of negative $\mathbb{Z}$ value are infinitesimal components (or vice versa).

Under this interpretation, we can say that the given closeness space is like a metric space, using the given field instead of $\mathbb{R}$ as the measure. It could be stated to use the 0 coordinate for the large plane, and the -1 coordinate for the miniature planes at each point of the large plan (in which case the space is interpreted as a roughly Euclidean plane with infinitesimal distances, or to use the 1-coordinate for the large plane, and the 0 coordinate for the small planes (in which case the space is interpreted as an infinite plane of real planes — it is to the Euclidean plane roughly as ω_2 is to ω among ordinals), or indeed z and $z - 1$ for any integer z.

Example 3.15.1: Non-Standard Analysis

This allows achievement of at least some of the results of nonstandard analysis. For example:

Definition 3.15.1.1:

  For the duration of this example, we define the nearest real number to a finite value to be the value of the same first coordinate, and zero component in the second coordinate. (I.e. a distance of 3.7×0 is the nearest real number to 3.7×-23.4. 3.7×-23.4 or 0×14 are not the nearest real numbers to anything.)

Definition 3.15.1.2:

  We define the limit of a function f at point x to be equal to the nearest real number to $f(x + \varepsilon)$, if such a real number exists and is uniquely defined across all infinitesimals ε.
  For example, the limit of $f(x) = x + 1$ at $x = 1$ is the nearest real number to

$f(x + \varepsilon) =$
$f(1 + \varepsilon) =$
$1 + \varepsilon + 1 =$
$2 + \varepsilon$

which has 2 as its nearest real number.

Definition 3.15.1.3:

  We define a function $f(x)$ to be continuous at point x if f is defined at x and if, for every infinitesimal e, we have $||f(x + \varepsilon) - f(x)||$ at most an infinitesimal.
  For example, if we have

$f(x) = x + 1$ if $x \geq 0$
$f(x) = 0$ otherwise

then we have f continuous at -1 and 1, but not continuous at 0:

$f(-1 + \varepsilon) - f(-1) = 0 - 0 f(1 + \varepsilon) - f(1) = 1 + \varepsilon + 1 - 1 + 1 = \varepsilon$

but problems when we examine a negative value of ε with nearest real number at 0:

If $\varepsilon < 0$, then $f(0 + \varepsilon) = f(\varepsilon)$, but we have f(0) = 0 + 1 = 1, and $0 - 1 = -1$ is not an infinitesimal.

Definition 3.15.1.4:

We define the derivative of a function f at point x to be the nearest real number to

$$(f(x + \varepsilon) - f(x)) / \varepsilon$$

if such a number exists and is well-defined across all infinitesimals ε.

For example, the derivative of $f(x) = x2$ is equal to the nearest real number to:

$((x + \varepsilon)2 - x2) / \varepsilon =$
$(x2 + 2x\varepsilon + \varepsilon2 - x2) / \varepsilon =$
$(2x\varepsilon + \varepsilon2) / \varepsilon =$
$2x + \varepsilon$

and the nearest real number to $2x + \varepsilon$ is 2x. So we have the derivative of x2 equal to 2x.

Closing remark

Providing a nonstandard analysis with derivatives seems straightforward enough; notwithstanding the fundamental theorem of calculus, it is not clear to this author how to adapt these findings to create an integral, although just as epsilon-delta arguments provide a finite workaround to infinitesimals, the core concept of integration in calculus finds a finite workaround to summation of an infinite number of infinitesimally thick slices. It might be noted that this system does yet have the infinite sums and infinite integers of non-standard analysis. Perhaps our restricted attention disregarded some closeness spaces or other matters yielding fields that would allow a more powerful non-standard analysis; perhaps work with the closeness spaces involving the ordinals cross $[0, 1)$ — a nonnegative long real number line — would achieve such things. However, we will draw a limit to the investigation here.

Discussion questions for "Closeness Spaces: An Elementary Introduction to Generalized Metric Spaces, and Ordered Fields Derived from Them"

1. What, if anything, does this dissertation tell a nontechnical audience about the author's early life?

2. What, if anything, does this dissertation tell a technical or mathematics audience about the author's early life?

3. What in this dissertation is unusual even within mathematics?

4. How interesting of a subbranch of mathematics is available given this dissertation?

Introduction to "Dark Patterns and Cultural Context Study of Scriptural Texts:
A Case Study in Craig Keener's Paul, Women, and Wives: Marriage and Women's Ministry in the Letters of Paul"

This piece scared off all other advisors, not because it uses a computer science concept inaccessible to a non-technical audience, but because I failed to adequately convey that a major concept in computer science (in this case, one originally from architecture) could be used in a humanities thesis and be understandable to humanities scholars.

As far as "religion and science" issues, this choice of topic may surprise a reader that has read the author's complaints about endemic misuse of "a term from science." This use of a concept from science arises from the author's formation and information technology experience, and so is not an orientalist-style import from an exotic field, but "Write about what you know."

This dissertation was written only a few months before the author was received into the Orthodox Church, and so it could be asserted that unusual features are not a strike against the author's Orthodoxy. However, the author sees little that he would change beyond the suggestion that the work is not (and has no pretensions to be) a true work of Orthodox theology, but a study of a trend and a style of rhetoric to be found in humanities disciplines, including Biblical studies, which takes problematic tertiary sources in Biblical studies and uses them as primary sources in addressing problematic rhetoric for which the author would later find a definitive how-to guide in Simon Lancaster's *Speechwriting: The Expert Guide.*

Dark Patterns and Cultural Context Study of Scriptural Texts: A Case Study in Craig Keener's *Paul, Women, and Wives: Marriage and Women's Ministry in the Letters of Paul*

Jonathan Hayward
christos.jonathan.hayward@gmail.com
CJSHayward.com

Diploma in Theology and Religious Studies, 2003
Faculty of Divinity
University of Cambridge
20 May 2003

Abstract

The author suggests how the concept of 'patterns' in architecture and computer science, or more specifically 'dark patterns' / 'anti-patterns', may provide a helpful vehicle to explicitly communicate tacit knowledge concerning problematic thought. The author also provides a pilot study which seeks to provide a sample analysis identifying indicators for the 'surprising cultural find' pattern in which cultural context is misused to explain away offending Bible passages.

Introduction to Patterns, Dark Patterns, and Anti-patterns

The technical concept of *pattern* is used in architecture and computer science, and the synonymous *dark patterns* and *anti-patterns* refer to patterns that are not recurring best practices so much as recurring pathologies; my encounter with them has been as a computer programmer in connection with the book nicknamed 'GoF'.[19] Patterns do not directly provide new knowledge about how to program; what they do provide is a way to take knowledge that expert practitioners share on a tacit level, and enable them both to discuss this knowledge amongst themselves and effectively communicate it to novice programmers. It is my belief that the concept is useful to Biblical studies in providing a way to discuss knowledge that is also held on a tacit level and is also beneficial to be able to discuss explicitly, and furthermore that dark patterns or anti-patterns bear direct relevance. I hope to give a brief summary of the concept of patterns,

---

[19] I.e. the 'Gang of Four': Gamma, Erich; Helm, Richard; Johnson, Ralph; Vlissides, John, *Design Patterns: Elements of Reusable Object-Oriented Software*, Boston: Addison-Wesley, 1994.

explaining their application to Biblical studies, then give a pilot study exploring one pattern, before some closing remarks.

Each pattern consists of a threefold rule, describing:

1. A context.

2. A set of forces within that context.

3. A resolution to those forces.

In the contexts of architecture and computer science, patterns are used to describe best practices which keep recurring and which embody a certain 'quality without a name'. I wish to make a different application, to identifying and describing certain recurring problematic ways of thought in Biblical or theological inquiry which may be understood as dark patterns, which often seem to be interlaced with sophistry and logical fallacy.

Two examples of what a dark pattern, or anti-pattern might be are the *consolation prize*, and the *surprising cultural find*. I would suggest that the following provide instances of the consolation prize: discussion of a spiritual resurrection, flowering words about the poetic truth of Genesis 1, and Calvin's eucharistic theology. If you speak of a spiritual resurrection that occurs instead of physical resurrection, you can draw Christians far more effectively than if you plainly say, 'I do not believe in Christ's physical resurrection.' The positive doctrine that is presented is a consolation prize meant to keep the audience from noticing what has been taken away. The context includes a text that (taken literally) a party wants to dismiss. The forces include the fact that Christians are normally hesitant to dismiss Scripture, and believe that insights can give them a changed and deepened understanding. The resolution is to dress up the dismissal of Scripture as a striking insight. Like other patterns, this need not be all reasoned out consciously; I suggest, via a quasi-Darwinian/meme propagation mechanism, that dismissals of Scripture that follow some such pattern are more likely to work (and therefore be encountered) than i.e. a dismissal of Scripture that is not merely undisguised but offensive.

In the surprising cultural find, a meticulous study is made of a passage's cultural context to find some basis to neutralise the passage so that its apparent meaning does not apply to us. The context is similar to that of the consolation prize, if more specific to a contemporary Western cultural setting. The forces, beyond those mentioned for the consolation prize, include ramifications of period awareness and the Standard Social Science Model: there is a very strong sense of how culture and period can influence people, and they readily believe claims about long ago and far away that which would seem fishy if said about people of our time and place. The resolution is to use the passage's cultural setting to produce disinformation: the fruits of careful scholarly research have turned up a surprising cultural find and the passage's apparent meaning does not apply to us. The passage may be presented, for instance, to mean something quite different from what it appears to mean, or to address a specific historical situation in a way that clearly does not apply to us.

It is the dark pattern of the surprising cultural find that I wish to investigate as a pilot case study in this thesis.

Case Study

Opening Comments

The aim of this case study is to provide a pilot study of how the surprising cultural find may be identified as a dark pattern. In so doing, I analyse one sample text closely, with reference to comparison texts when helpful.

I use the terms *yielding* to refer to analysis from scholars who presumably have interests but allow the text to contradict them, and *unyielding* to refer to analysis that will not allow the text to contradict the scholar's interests. Yielding analysis does not embody the surprising cultural find dark pattern, while unyielding analysis does. I consider the boundary to be encapsulated by the question, 'Is the text allowed to say "No!" to a proposed position?'

Ideally, one would compare two scholarly treatments that are alike in every fashion save that one is yielding and the other is unyielding. Finding a comparison text, I believe, is difficult because I was searching for a yielding text with the attributes of one that was unyielding. Lacking a perfect pair, I chose Peter T. O'Brien's *The Letter to the Ephesians*[20] and Bonnie Thurston's *Reading Colossians, Ephesians & 2 Thessalonians: A Literary and Theological Commentary*[21] to represent yielding analysis and Craig Keener's *Paul, Women, Wives: Marriage and Women's Ministry in the Letters of Paul* [22] to represent unyielding analysis. I was interested in treatment of Ephesians 5:21-33. When I use Biblical references without a book, I will always be referring to Ephesians. All three of secondary sources present themselves as making the fruits of scholarly research accessible to the layperson. O'Brien provides an in-depth, nonfeminist commentary. Thurston provides a concise, feminist commentary. Keener provides an in-depth, Biblical Egalitarian monograph. Unfortunately, the ordered copy of Thurston did not arrive before external circumstances precluded the incorporation of new materials (and may have been misidentified, meaning that my advisor and I both failed after extensive searching to find a yielding feminist or egalitarian treatment of the text). My study is focused on Keener with comparison to O'Brien where expedient.

[20] Leicester: Apollos, 1999.
[21] Macon: Smyth & Helwys, 1999.

[22] Peabody: Hendrickson, 1992.

There seems to be an interconnected web of distinguishing features to these dark patterns, laced with carefully woven sophistry, and there are several dimensions on which a text may be examined. The common-sense assumption that these features are all independent of each other seems to be debatable. One example of this lack of independence is the assumption that what an author believes is independent of whether the analysis is yielding: the suboptimal comparison texts were selected partly because of the difficulty a leading Christians for Biblical Equality scholar and I experienced trying to locate yielding feminist analyses other than Thurston in Tyndale's library. I do not attempt to seriously investigate the interconnections, beyond commenting that features seem interconnected and less independent of each other than most scholars would assume by default.

The substance of my inquiry focuses on observable attributes of the text. I believe that before that point, observing a combination of factors may provide cues. I will mention these factors, but not develop them; there are probably others:

- Is the book a monograph organised around one of today's hot issues, or e.g. a commentary organised around the contents of a Biblical text?

- If you just open the book to its introduction, do you meet forceful persuasion? Are those first pages written purely to persuade, or do they attempt other endeavours (e.g. give factual or theoretical background that is not especially polemical)? What is the approach to persuasion?

- Does the book contain anything besides cultural arguments finding that Biblical texts which apparently contradict the author's camp need not be interpreted that way?

- How much does the author appear able to question our Zeitgeist (in a direction other than a more thorough development of assumptions in our Zeitgeist)?

- What, in general, does the publisher try to do? The publisher is not the author, but publishers have specific aims and goals. It would seem to require explanation to say that a company indiscriminately publishes yielding and unyielding analysis because both resonate equally well with its editorial climate.

There will be a decided imbalance between attention paid to Keener and O'Brien. Part of this is due to external constraints, and part is due to a difference between O'Brien and Keener. With one major exception, described shortly, O'Brien's analysis doesn't run afoul of the concern I am exploring. If I were writing cultural commentary for my texts as Keener and O'Brien write cultural commentary for their texts, I would ideally spend as much time explaining the backgrounds to what Keener and O'Brien said. I believe they are both thinkers who were shaped by, draw on, and are critical of their cultures and subcultures. Explaining what they said, as illuminated by their context, would require parity in treatment. However, I do not elaborate their teachings set in context, but explore a problem that is far more present in Keener than in O'Brien or Thurston. I have more of substance to say about how Keener exhibits a problem than how O'Brien doesn't. As such, after describing a problem, I might give a footnote reference to a passage in O'Brien which shows *some* analogy without seeming to exhibit the problem under discussion, but I will not systematically attempt to make references to O'Brien's yielding analysis as wordy as explanations of Keener's unyielding analysis.

The one significant example of unyielding analysis noted in O'Brien is in the comment on 5:21: O'Brien notes that reciprocal submission is not enjoined elsewhere in the Bible, points out that 'allelous' occurs in some contexts that do not lend themselves to reciprocal reading ('so that men should slay one another'[23]), and concludes that 'Believers, submit to one another,' means only that lower-status Christians should submit to those placed above them. This is as problematic as other instances of unyielding analysis, and arguably more disturbing as it lacks some of the common indicators alerting the careful reader to be suspicious. There is a point of contact between this treatment and Keener's: both assume that 5:21 and 5:22-6:9 are not merely connected but are saying the same thing, and it is one thing only. It is assumed that the text cannot enjoin of us both symmetrical and asymmetrical submission, so one must be the *real* commandment, and the other is explained away. Both Keener and O'Brien end up claiming that something is commanded in 5:21 with clarificatory examples following, without asserting that either 5:21 or 5:22-6:9 says something substantively different from the other about submission. I will not further analyse this passage beyond this mention: I consider it a clear example of unyielding analysis. This is the one part of O'Brien I have read of which I would not say, '...and this is an example of analogous concerns addressed by yielding scholarship.'

The introductions to O'Brien and Keener provided valuable cues as to the tone subsequently taken by the texts. Both are written to persuade a claim that some of their audience rejects, but the divergence in how they seek to persuade is significant. Keener's introduction is written to persuade the reader of Biblical Egalitarianism: in other words, of a position on one of today's current issues. The beginning of O'Brien's introduction tries to persuade the reader of Pauline authorship for Ephesians, which they

---

[23] Rev. 6:8, RSV.

acknowledge to be an unusual position among scholars today; the introduction is not in any direct sense about today's issues. O'Brien's introduction is written both to persuade and introduce the reader to scholarly perspectives on background; while nontechnical, it is factually dense and heavy with footnotes. Keener's introduction seems to be written purely to persuade: he give statistics[24] concerning recent treatment of women which are highly emotionally charged, no attempt being made to connect them to the text or setting of the Pauline letters. Keener's introduction uses emotion to bypass rationality, using loaded language and various other forms of questionable persuasion explored below; a naive reader first encountering this debate in Keener's introduction could well wonder how any compassionate person could be in the other camp. O'Brien works to paint a balanced picture, and gives a fair account of the opposing view before explaining why he considers it inadequate. O'Brien seeks to persuade through logical argument, and his book's pages persuade (or fail to persuade) as the reader finds his arguments to be sufficient (or insufficient) reason to accept its conclusions.

Emotional Disinformation

Among the potential indicators found in Keener, the first broad heading I found could be described as *factual disinformation* and *emotional disinformation*. 'Disinformation', as used in military intelligence, ordinarily denotes deception through careful presentation of true details; I distinguish 'factual disinformation' (close to 'disinformation' traditionally understood) from 'emotional disinformation', which is disinformation that acts on emotional and compassionate judgment as factual disinformation acts on factual judgment. While

[24] Keener, pp. 7-9.

conceptually distinct, they seem tightly woven in the text, and I do not attempt to separate them.

An Emotional Plea

One distinguishing feature of Keener's introduction is that it closes off straightforward rebuttal. Unlike O'Brien, he tries to establish not only the content of debate but the terms of debate itself, and once Keener has established the terms of debate, it is difficult or impossible to argue the opposing view from within those terms. Rebuttal *is* possible, of course, but here it would seem to require pushing the discussion back one notch in the meta-level hierarchy and arguing at much greater length. O'Brien seems more than fair in his style of argument; Keener loads the dice before his reader knows what is going on.

One passage is worth citing for close study:[25]

> There are issues where most Biblically conservative Christians, including myself, disagree with prominent elements of the feminist movement... But there are other concerns which nearly all Christians, including myself, and nearly the whole women's movement plainly share....
>
> [Approximately two pages of alarming claims and statistics, including:] ...Although "bride-burning" is now illegal in India, it still happens frequently; a bride whose dowry is insufficient may be burned to death so that her husband can find a new partner. There is no investigation, of course, because it is said that she simply poured cooking oil over herself and set herself on fire accidentally.... A

---

[25] *Ibid.*, pp. 6-9; compare almost any of O'Brien pp. 4-47.

Rhode Island Rape Crisis Center study of 1700
teenagers, cited in a 1990 InterVarsity
magazine, reported that 65% of the boys and
47% of the girls in sixth through ninth grades
say that a man may force a woman to have sex
with him if they've been dating for more than
six months.... Wife-beating seems to have
been a well-established practice in many
patriarchal families of the 1800's....

But while some Christians may once have
been content to cite proof-texts about
women's subordination to justify ignoring this
sort of oppression, virtually all of us would
today recognise that oppression and
exploitation of any sort are sinful violations of
Jesus's commandment to love our neighbour
as ourselves and to love fellow-Christians as
Christ loved us. [Keener goes on to later
conclude that we must choose between a
feminist conception of equality and an un-
Christian version of subordination.]

The text starts by presenting Keener as Biblically
conservative, moves to a heart-wrenching list of wrongs
against women, implicitly conflates nonfeminist Christians
with those who condone rape and murder, and presents a
choice crystallising the fallacy of the excluded middle that
had been lurking in prior words. It has more than one
attribute of emotional disinformation.
    Keener both identifies himself as Biblically
conservative and says that, among some Christians, the
egalitarian position is the conservative one (contrast
chapter 4, where 'conservative' means a reactionary
misogynist). Why? People are more likely to listen to
someone who is perceivedly of the same camp, and falsely

claiming membership in your target's camp is a tool of deceptive persuasion.

The recitation of statistics is interesting for several reasons.

On a strictly logical level, it is a non sequitur. It has no direct logical bearing on either camp; even its rhetorical position assumes that conservative, as well as liberal, members of his audience believe that rape and murder are atrocities. This is a logical non sequitur, chosen for its emotional force and what impact that emotional recoil will have on susceptibility. The trusting reader will recoil from the oppression listed and be less guarded when Keener provides his way to oppose such oppression. The natural response to such a revolting account is to say, 'I'm not that! I'm the opposite!' and embrace what is offered when the fallacy of the excluded middle is made explicit, in the choice Keener later presents.

Once a presentation of injustice has aroused compassion to indignation, most people do not use their full critical faculties: they want to right a wrong, not sit and analyse. This means that a powerful account of injustice (with your claims presented as a way to fight the injustice) is a powerful way to get people to accept claims that would be rejected if presented on their logical merits. Keener's 'of course' is particularly significant; he builds the reader's sense of outrage by adding 'of course' with a (carefully studied but) seemingly casual manner. It is not obvious to a Western reader that a bride's murder would be left uninvestigated; adding 'of course' gives nothing to Keener's logical case but adds significantly to the emotional effect Keener seeks, more effectively and more manipulatively than were he to visibly write those words from outrage.

The sentence about proof-texts and loving one's neighbour is of particular interest. On a logical level, it is restrained and cannot really be attacked. The persuasive and emotional force—distinct from what is logically present—is closer to, 'Accepting those proof-texts is

equivalent to supporting such oppression; following the
Law of Love contradicts both.'

This is one instance of a broader phenomenon: a gap
between what the author *entails* and *implicates*. Both
'entail' and 'implicate' are similar in meaning to 'imply', but
illustrate opposite sides of a distinction. What a text *entails*
is what is implied by the text in a strictly logical sense; what
a text *implicates* is what is implied in the sense of what it
leads the reader to believe. What is implicated includes
what is entailed, and may often include other things. The
entailed content of 'But while some Christians...' is modest
and does not particularly advance a discussion of
egalitarianism. The implicated content is much more
significant; it takes a logically tight reading to recognise that
the text does not entail a conflation claiming that
nonfeminist Christians condone rape and murder. The text
implicates much more than it entails, and I believe that this
combination of restricted entailment with far-reaching
implication is a valuable cue. *It can be highly informative
to read a text with an eye to the gap between what is
entailed and what is implicated.* The gap between
entailment and implicature seemed noticeably more
pronounced in Keener than in yielding materials I have
read, including O'Brien. Another example of a gap between
entailment and implicature is found close,[26] '...the secular
generalization that Christians (both men and women) who
respect the Bible oppose women's rights is an inaccurate
caricature of these Christians' admits a similar analysis: the
entailment is almost unassailable, while the implicature
establishes in the reader's mind that the conservative
position is excisable from respect for the Bible, and that the
nonfeminist position denies something basic to women that
they should have. The term 'women's rights' is by
entailment the sort of thing one would not want to oppose,
and by implicature a shorthand for 'women's rights as

[26] Keener, p. 9.

understood and interpreted along feminist lines'. As well as showing a significant difference between entailment and implicature, this provides an example of a text which closes off the most obvious means of rebuttal, another rhetorical trait which may be produced by the same mindset as produces unyielding analysis.

What is left out of the cited text is also significant. The statistics given are incomplete (they focus on profound ways in which women suffer so the reader will not think of profound ways in which men suffer) but as far as describing principles to discriminate yielding versus unyielding analysis, this seems to be privileged information. I don't see a way to let a reader compare the text as if there were a complementary account written in the margin. Also, a careful reading of the text may reveal a Biblical nonfeminist position as the middle fallaciously excluded earlier, in which sexual distinction exists on some basis *other* than violence. All texts we are interested in—yielding or unyielding—must stop somewhere, but it is possible to exclude data that should have been included and try to conceal its absence. Lacunae that seem to have been chosen for persuasion rather than limitation of scope may signal unyielding analysis.

Further Examples

In a discussion[27] of the *haustafel's* (Ephesians 5:21 and following[28] injunction that the husband love his wife based on Christ's love for the Church, Keener says, 'Indeed, Christ's love is explicitly defined in this passage in terms of self-sacrificial service, not in terms of his authority.' The passage does not mention that self-sacrificial service is a defining feature of Christ's model of authority, and in these pages the impression is created that the belief in servant

---

[27] *Ibid.*, p. 167.
[28] A *haustafel* is a household code such as the one found in Ephesians; for my purposes, the Ephesians haustafel stretches from 5:21 to 6:9.

love is a Biblical Egalitarian distinctive, so that the reader
might be surprised to find the conservative *O'Brien*
saying:[29]

> ...Paul does not here, or anywhere else for that
> matter, exhort husbands to rule over their
> wives. They are nowhere told, 'Exercise your
> headship!' Instead, they are urged repeatedly
> to love their wives (vv. 25, 28, and 33). This
> will involve each husband showing unceasing
> care and loving service for his wife's entire
> well-being...

O'Brien is emphatic that husbands must love their
wives; examples could easily be multiplied. Keener argues
for loving servanthood as if it were a claim which his
opponents rejected. The trusting reader will believe that
nonfeminists believe in submission and egalitarians alone
recognise that Paul calls husbands to servant love. I believe
that this selective fact-telling is one of the more
foundational indicators: some factual claims will be out of a
given reader's competence to evaluate, but so far as a reader
can evaluate whether a fair picture is presented, the
presence or absence of selective fact-telling may help.

Chapter 4 is interesting in that there are several
thoughts that are very effectively conveyed without being
explicitly stated. The account of 'conservatives' (i.e.
misogynistic reactionaries) is never explicitly stated to
apply to Christians who disagree with Keener, but works in
a similar fashion (and for similar reasons) to the 'Green
Book' which introduces the first major argument in The
Abolition of Man.[30] By the same mechanism as the Green
Book leads the reader to believe that claims about the outer
world are in fact only claims about ourselves, not the

[29] O'Brien, p. 419.
[30] Lewis, C.S., chapter 1, pp. 1-26, San Francisco: Harper San Francisco, 1943, 2001.

slightest obstacle is placed to the reader believing that Keener exposes the true nature of 'conservatism', and that the picture of Graeco-Roman conservatism portrayed is a picture of *conservatism*, period, as true of conservatism today as ever.

A smaller signal may be found in that Keener investigates inconvenient verses in a way that never occurs for convenient ones. Keener explores the text, meaning, and setting to 5:22-33 in a way that never occurs for 5:21; a careless reader may get the impression that 5:21 doesn't *have* a cultural setting.

Drawing on Privileged Information

I would next like to outline a difference between men's and women's communication, state what Keener's Roman conservatives did with this, and state what Keener did with the Roman conservatives. One apparent gender difference in communication is that when a woman makes a claim, it is relatively likely to mean, 'I am in the process of thinking and here is where I am now,' while a man's claim is more likely to mean, 'I have thought. I have come to a conclusion. Here is my conclusion.' Without mentioning caveats, there is room for *considerable* friction when men assume that women are stating conclusions and women assume that men are giving the current state of a developing thought. The conservatives described by Keener seem frustrated by this friction; Keener quotes Josephus:[31]

> Put not trust in a single witness, but let there
> be three or at least two, whose evidence shall

---

[31] Keener, p. 163; O'Brien in pp. 405-438 does not cite a non-Biblical primary source likely to be similarly repellent, and portrays opposing secondary sources as mistaken without setting them in a disturbing light, i.e. in footnote 211, page 413.

be accredited by their past lives. From women let no evidence be accepted, because of the levity and temerity of their sex; neither let slaves bear witness, because of the baseness of their soul.

This passage is introduced, "...regards the prohibition of women's testimony as part of God's law, based in the moral inferiority inherent in their gender." The reader is not likely to question whether it's *purely* misogyny for a man (frustrated by women apparently showing levity by changing their minds frequently) to find this perceived mutability a real reason why these people should not be relied on as witnesses when someone's life may be at stake. Keener has been working to portray conservatives as misogynistic. Two pages earlier,[32] he tells us,

An early Jewish teacher whose work was undoubtedly known to Paul advised men not to sit among women, because evil comes from them like a moth emerging from clothes. A man's evil, this teacher went on to complain, is better than a woman's good, for she brings only shame and reproach.

This, and other examples which could be multiplied, deal with something crystallised on the previous page.[33] Keener writes,

Earlier philosophers were credited with a prayer of gratitude that they were not born women, and a century after Paul a Stoic emperor could differentiate a women's soul from that of a man.

[32] Keener, p. 161.
[33] *Ibid.*, p. 160.

The moral of this story is that believing in nonphysical differences between men and women is tantamount to misogyny. This is a highly significant claim, given that the questions of women's ordination and headship in marriage are largely epiphenomenal to the question of whether we are created masculine and feminine at every level of our being, or ontologically neuter spirits in reproductively differentiated bodies. Keener produces a conclusion (i.e. that the human spirit is neuter) *without ever stating it or drawing the reader to consciously consider* whether this claim should be believed. In a text that is consistently polite, the opposing view is not merely negated but vilified: to hold this view (it is portrayed) is tantamount to taking a view of women which is extraordinarily reprehensible. Either of these traits may signal unyielding analysis; I believe the combination is particularly significant.

Tacit and Overt Communication

Although the full import of tacit versus overt communication is well beyond my competency to address, I would like to suggest something that merits further study.[34] Keener seemed, to a significant degree, to:

---

[34] My attempts to find material discussing how these things work, academic or popular, have had mixed success. If I were to write a thesis around this issue, I would initially explore works such as Michael I. Polanyi's *Personal Knowledge: Towards a Post-Critical Philosophy*, Chicago: University of Chicago Press, 1958, and anthropological treatments of the high-context/low-context and direct/indirect axes of human communication (which suggest relevant lines of inquiry). C.S. Lewis's account of the Unman's dialogue with the Lady in *Perelandra* (chapters 8-11, pp. 274-311 in *Out of the Silent Planet / Perelandra*, Surrey: Voyager Classics, 1938 / 1943), seems to represent a very perceptive grappling with the issue of tacit communication in relation to deceit.

- *Tacitly convey most of his important points*, without stating them explicitly.

- *Present claims so the opposing view is never considered.*

- *Build up background assumptions which will produce the desired conclusions, more than give explicit arguments.*

- *Work by manipulating background assumptions, often provided by the reader's culture.*

As an example of this kind of tacit communication, I would indicate two myths worked with in the introduction and subsequently implied. By 'myth' I do not specifically mean 'widespread misconception', but am using a semiotic term comparable in meaning to 'paradigm': '[M]yths act as scanning devices of a society's *'possibles'* and *'pensables.'*[35] The two myths are:

- *Men are powerful and violent aggressors, whilst women are powerless and innocent victims.* The alarming claims and statistics[36] mention aggression against men only in the most incidental fashion.

- *The accurate spokesperson for women's interests is the feminist movement.* Keener diminishes this myth's force by disclaiming support for abortion (and presenting a pro-choice stance as separable from other feminist claims), but (even when decrying prenatal discrimination in sex-selective abortion)[37]

[35] Maranda, Pierre, 'Elusive Semiosis', *The Semiotic Review of Books*, Volume 3, Issue 1, seen in 2003 at
http://www.bdk.rug.nl/onderzoek/castor/srb/srb/elusive.html.
[36] Keener, pp. 7-9.
[37] *Ibid.*, p. 7.

Keener refers to the feminist movement interchangeably as 'the feminist movement'[38] and 'the women's movement',[39] and does not lead the reader to consider that one could speak for women's interests by contradicting feminism, or question the *a priori* identification of womens' interests with the content of feminist claims.

Argument Structure

As well as the emotional disinformation explored in many of the examples above, there are several points where the nature of the argument is of interest. Five argument-like features are explored:

- o Verses which help our position are principles that apply across all time; verses which contradict our position were written to address specific issues in a specific historical context.

- o X had beneficial effect Y; X was therefore purely instrumental to Y, and we may remove X if we no longer require X as an instrument to Y.

- o The absolute position taken in this passage addresses a specific historical idiosyncrasy, but the relative difference between this passage and its surroundings is a timeless principle across all times.

- o If X resonates with a passage's cultural context, then X need not be seen as part of the

[38] *Ibid.*, p. 6.
[39] *Ibid.*, p. 9.

Bible's revelation.

- o We draw the lines of equivalence in the
  following manner...

'Verses which help our position are principles that
apply across all time; verses which contradict our position
were written to address specific issues in a specific
historical context' is less an argument than an emergent
property. It's not argued; the text just turns out that way.
Keener gives a diplomatically stated reason why Paul wrote
the parts of 5:22-6:9 he focuses on: 'Paul was very smart.'[40]
The subsequent argument states that Paul wrote in a
context where Christians behaving conservatively would
diminish he perceived threat to social conservatives. Keener
writes,[41] 'Paul is responding to a specific cultural issue for
the sake of the Gospel, and his words should not be taken at
face value in all cultures.' There is a fallacy which seems to
be behind this argument in Keener: being timeless
principles and being historically prompted are non-
overlapping categories, so finding a historical prompt
suffices to demonstrate that material in question does not
display a timeless principle.
      'X had beneficial effect Y; X was therefore purely
instrumental to Y, and we may remove X if we no longer
require X as an instrument to Y.' Keener argues[42] that the
haustafel mitigated prejudice against Christianity, which is
presented as a reason why we need not observe the

---

[40] *Ibid.*, p. 141. Contrast O'Brien's comments on 6:5-9 in 447-456,
    seemingly the most obvious place to portray at least *some* of the text
    as parochial; O'Brien disclaims that Paul was making any social
    comment on slavery (p. 448), but unpacks the verses without
    obviously approaching the text from the same mindset as Keener.
[41] Keener, p. 170.
[42] *Ibid.*, pp. 174-8. O'Brien covers some of the same basic facts without
    obviously presenting argument in this vein (pp. 405-409).

haustafel if we do not perceive need for that apologetic concern.

'The absolute position taken in this passage addresses a specific historical idiosyncrasy, but the relative difference between this passage and its surroundings is a timeless principle across all times.' A text embodies both an absolute position *in se*, and a relative difference by how it is similar to and different from its surrounding cultural mainstream. 5:22-33 requires submission of wives and love of husbands; that absolute position can be understood with little study of context, while the relative difference showed both a continuity with Aristotelian *haustafels* and a difference by according women a high place that was unusual in its setting. The direction of Keener's argument is to say explicitly[43] that the verses should not be taken at face value, and to implicitly clarify that the absolute position should not be taken at face value, but *part* of the relative position, namely the sense in which Paul was much more feminist-like than his setting ('[A quote from Plutarch] is one of the most "progressive" social models in Paul's day... It is most natural to read Paul as making a much more radical statement than Plutarch, both because of what Paul says and because of what he does not say,'[44]) *is* a timeless principle that should apply in our day as well as Paul's. Without proper explanation of why the relative difference should be seen as absolute, given that the absolute position is idiosyncratic, the impression is strongly conveyed that respecting Paul's spirit means transposing his absolute position so that a similar relative difference exists with relation to our setting.

'If X resonates with a passage's cultural context, then X need not be seen as part of the Bible's revelation.' This is often interwoven with the previous two arguments. Apart from showing a feminist-like relative difference, Keener

---

[43] Keener, p. 170.
[44] *Ibid.*, p. 170.

works to establish that Paul used a *haustafel* in a way that
reduced Christianity's perceived threat to conservatives.
This is presented as establishing that therefore wives are
not divinely commanded to submit.

'We draw equivalences in the following manner...'
This is not a single argument so much as an attribute of
arguments; I believe that what is presented as equivalent
can be significant. In the autobiographical comments in the
introduction, Keener writes[45]:

> "But it's part of the Bible!" I protested. "If you
> throw this part out, you have to throw
> everything else out, too." I cannot recall
> anyone having a good response to my
> objection, but even as a freshman I knew very
> well that if I were consistent in my stance
> against using culture to interpret the Bible, I
> would have to advocate women's head
> coverings in church, the practice of holy
> kisses, and parentally arranged marriages.

What Keener has been arguing is not just the
relevance of culture but the implicit necessity of a piecemeal
hermeneutic. The implication (beyond an excluded middle)
is that using culture to argue a piecemeal, feminist
modification to Paul is the same sort of thing as not literally
practicing the holy kiss.[46] The sixth of seven chapters, after

---

[45] *Ibid.*, p. 4; contrast the series preface before O'Brien: 'God stands
over against us; we do not stand in judgment of him. When God
speaks to us through his Word, those who profess to know him
must respond in an appropriate way...' (page viii).

[46] Remember that Keener is an American. The suggestion he makes is
more significant in U.S. than English culture. U.S. culture has a
place for giving kisses to one's romantic partner, to family, and to
small children, but not ordinarily to friends. Because of this, culture
shock affects almost any attempt to consider ecclesiastical usage.
'Greet one another with a holy kiss.' serves in U.S. Evangelical
conversation as the standard example of a New Testament

emotionally railing against slavery, argues that retaining the institution of marriage while excising one dimension is the same sort of thing as abolishing the institution of slavery; 'The Obedience of Children: A Better Model?'[47] explicitly rejects the claim that marriage is more like parenthood than owning slaves. While no comparison is perfect, I believe that these are examples of comparisons where it is illuminating to see what the author portrays as equivalent.

In some cases, the argument types I have described are not things which must be wrong, but things which lack justification. The claim that an absolute position is parochial but the relative difference is timeless is not a claim I consider to be unjustifiable, but it is a claim which I believe *requires* justification, a justification which is not necessarily provided.

In my own experience at least, this kind of argument is not purely the idiosyncrasy of one book. The idea this thesis is based on occurred to me after certain kinds of arguments recurred. Certain dark patterns, or anti-patterns, came up in different contexts like a broken record that kept on making its sound. I'm not sure how many times I had seen instances of 'X had beneficial effect Y; X was therefore purely instrumental to Y, and we may remove X if we no longer require X as an instrument to Y,' but I did *not* first meet that argument in Keener. These arguments represent fallacies of a more specialised nature than *post hoc, ergo propter hoc* ("after the fact, therefore because of the fact") or *argumentum ad ignorantiam* ("appeal to ignorance"). I believe that they allow a persuasive, rational-seeming

injunction which cannot be taken seriously as a commandment to follow. It seems to be often assumed as an example of cultural noise in the Bible.

[47] Keener, pp. 186-188; contrast O'Brien, pp. 409-438, where he elaborates the text's analogy with Christ and the Church as a model for understanding marriage, rather than comparing to slavery (which Keener not only does but works to give the reader a reservoir of anger at slavery which may transfer when he argues that marital submission is like slavery).

argument of a conclusion not yet justified on logical terms. The experience that led to the formation of my thesis was partly from repeatedly encountering such fallacies in surprising cultural find arguments.

Conclusion

I have tried to provide a pilot study identifying indicators of unyielding analysis. These indicators are not logically tied in the sense of 'Here's something which, on logical terms, can only indicate unyielding analysis.' The unyielding analysis I have met, before and in Keener, has been constructed with enough care to logic that I don't start by looking at logic. There are other things which are not of logical necessity required by unyielding analysis, but which seem to be produced by the same mindset. I have encountered these things both in the chosen text and in repeated previous experiences which first set me thinking along these lines.

At a fairly basic level, the case study is a study of a cultural dimension of communication. I believe that portions of this pilot study may be deepened by the insights of scholars from humanities which study human culture and communication. I believe that some of my remarks would be improved by a serious attempt to connect them with high-context and low-context communication as studied in anthropology. If I am doing a pilot study that cannot provide much of any firm answers, I do hope to suggest fruitful lines of inquiry and identify deep questions which for which interdisciplinary study could be quite fruitful.

It is unfortunate that my control text made little use of emotion. I believe my case study would have been better rounded, had I been able to contrast emotion subverting logic in Keener with emotion complementing logic in the control text. As it is, the case study lends itself to an unfortunate reading of "logic is good and emotion is bad", and gives the impression that I consider the bounds of legitimate persuasion to simply be those of logic.

On a broader scale, it is my hope that this may serve not only as a pilot study regarding unyielding analysis but a tentative introduction of a modified concept of 'pattern', or rather 'dark pattern' or 'anti-pattern' in theology. The concept of pattern was introduced by the architect Christopher Alexander and is sufficiently flexible to be recognised as powerful in computer science. I believe there are other patterns that can be helpful, and I would suggest that books like Alexander's *The Timeless Way of Building*[48] are accessible to people in a number of disciplines.

Directions for Further Inquiry

There were other indicators which I believe could be documented from this text with greater inquiry, but which I have not investigated due to constraints. Among these may be mentioned:

- o *Misrepresentation of material.* Recognising this would seem to require privileged information, and work better for an area where the reader knows something rather than nothing, but I believe that a reader who knows part of the covered domain stands to benefit from seeing if it is covered fairly.

- o *Doing more than a text presents itself as doing.* A certain kind of deceit, in which the speaker works hard to preserve literal truth, has a complex quality caused by more going on than is presented. I believe an exploration of this quality, and its tie to unyielding

[48] Oxford: Oxford University Press, 1979.

analysis, may be fruitful.

- ○ *Shared attributes with a test case.* A small
  and distinctive minority of cases qualify to
  become test cases in American legal practice;
  they possess a distinct emotional signature,
  and portions of Keener's argument (i.e.
  'Would [Paul] have ignored her personal
  needs in favour of the church's witness?')[49] are
  reminiscent in both argument and emotional
  appeal of test cases.

- ○ *An Amusement Park Ride with a Spellbinding
  Showman.* Especially in their introductions,
  O'Brien seems to go out of his way to let the
  reader know the full background to the
  debate; Keener seems more like a fascinating
  showman who directs the reader's attention to
  certain things *and away from others*;
  knowing the other side to statistics cited[50]—or
  even knowing that there *is* another side—
  destroys the effect. A careful description of
  this difference in rhetoric may be helpful, and
  I believe may be tied to disinformation in that
  there is a difference in working style; yielding
  persuasion suffers far less from the reader
  knowing the other side than does unyielding
  persuasion.

  More broadly, I believe there is room for inquiry into
the relation between this use of patterns and that in other
disciplines. The application I have made is not a straight
transposition; in architecture and computer science
patterns are a tool to help people communicate about best

[49] Keener, p. 148.
[50] *Ibid.* pp. 7-8.

practices to follow, not identify questionable practice to criticise as I have done here. What becomes of the Quality Without a Name may be interesting. This thesis only suggests two patterns; GoF[51] describes twenty-three computer programming patterns broken into three groups, so that they provide a taxonomy of recurring solutions and not merely a list. A taxonomy of Biblical studies patterns could be a valuable achievement.

Lastly, I would suggest that a study of *sharpening* and *leveling* would be fruitful.[52] 'Sharpening' and 'leveling' refer to a phenomenon where people remembering a text tend to sharpen its main points while leveling out attenuating factors. For many texts, sharpening and leveling are an unintended effect of their publication, while Keener seems at times to write to produce a specific result after sharpening and leveling have taken effect. What he writes *in itself* is more carefully restrained than what a reader would walk away thinking, and the latter appears to be closer to what Keener wants to persuade the reader of. Combining narrow entailment with broad implicature is a way for an author to write a text that creates a strong impression (sharpening and leveling produce an impression from what is implicated more than what is entailed) while being

---

[51] I.e. the 'Gang of Four': Gamma, Erich; Helm, Richard; Johnson, Ralph; Vlissides, John, *Design Patterns: Elements of Reusable Object-Oriented Software*, Boston: Addison-Wesley, 1994.

[52] Comments from Asher Koriat, Morris Goldsmith, and Ainat Pansky in 'Toward a Psychology of Memory Accuracy (in the 2000 *Annual Review of Psychology* as seen in 2003 at http://www.findarticles.com/cf_0/m0961/2000_Annual/6185563 5/p7/article.jhtml?term=) provide a summary, with footnotes, suggesting the basic psychological mechanism. An accessible treatment of a related, if not identical, application to what I suggest here is found on pp. 91-94 in Thomas Gilovich's *How We Know What Isn't So*, New York: The Free Press, 1993.

[Comment added in 2022: An in-depth, how-to manual for Keener's style of communication may be found in Lancaster, Simon, *Speechwriting: The Expert Guide* (Hale Expert Guides), London: Robert Hale 2011.]

relatively immune to direct criticism: when a critic rereads a text closely, it turns out that the author didn't really say the questionable things the critic remembers the author to have said.

Discussion questions for "Dark Patterns and Cultural Context Study of Scriptural Texts: A Case Study in Craig Keener's *Paul, Women, and Wives: Marriage and Women's Ministry in the Letters of Paul*"

1. Is there much straight shooting in Keener's text?

2. Is there much straight shooting in feminism?

3. Is dirty persuasion here connected with dirty persuasion in feminism as a whole?

4. What does this say about whether we should be believing in feminism?

Introduction to "AI as an Arena for Magical Thinking Among Skeptics"

The rumor mill has it that we're making real progress in AI, and full AI is just around the corner. The rumor mill, as usual, is wrong, and not just for reasons discussed in "Just Around the Corner Since 1950."

The AI movement has created some interesting capacities, but this dissertation offers a theological critique of the artificial intelligence movement as a whole. The critique gives an overview of ranges of critiques of the AI movement that are not offered in mainstream critiques because they lie too close to the camp they oppose.

The previous dissertation makes use of a concept used in computer science to inform a "handmaiden of theology" study. This uses theological concepts to form an incisive critique of AI as bad and sometimes very wishful thinking that doesn't produce the results it is trying to produce.

AI as an Arena for Magical Thinking Among Skeptics

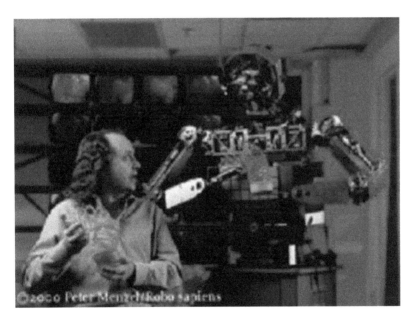

©2000 Peter Menzel/Robo sapiens

M.Phil. Dissertation
Jonathan Hayward
christos.jonathan.hayward@gmail.com
CJSHayward.com
15 June 2004

Table of Contents

Abstract

I explore artificial intelligence as failing in a way that is characteristic of a faulty anthropology. Artificial intelligence has had excellent funding, brilliant minds, and exponentially faster computers, which suggests that any failures present may not be due to lack of resources, but arise from an error that is manifest in anthropology and may even be cosmological. Maximus Confessor provides a genuinely different background to criticise artificial intelligence, a background which shares far fewer assumptions with the artificial intelligence movement than figures like John Searle. Throughout this dissertation, I will be looking at topics which seem to offer something interesting, even if cultural factors today often obscure their relevance. I discuss Maximus's use of the patristic distinction between 'reason' and spiritual 'intellect' as providing an interesting alternative to 'cognitive faculties.' My approach is meant to be distinctive both by reference to Greek Fathers and by studying artificial intelligence in light of the occult foundations of modern science, an important datum omitted in the broader scientific movement's self-presentation. The occult serves as a bridge easing the transition between Maximus Confessor's worldview and that of artificial intelligence. The broader goal is to make three suggestions: first, that artificial intelligence provides an experimental test of scientific materialism's picture of the human mind; second, that the outcome of the experiment suggests we might reconsider scientific materialism's I-It relationship to the world; and third, that figures like Maximus Confessor, working within an I-Thou relationship, offer more wisdom to us today than is sometimes assumed. I do not attempt to compare Maximus Confessor's Orthodoxy with other religious traditions, however I do suggest that Orthodoxy has relevant insights into personhood which the artificial intelligence community still lacks.

Introduction

Some decades ago, one could imagine a science fiction writer asking, 'What would happen if billions of dollars, dedicated laboratories with some of the world's most advanced equipment, indeed an important academic discipline with decades of work from some of the world's most brilliant minds—what if all of these were poured into an attempt to make an artificial mind based on an understanding of personhood that came out of a framework of false assumptions?' We could wince at the waste, or wonder that after all the failures the researchers still had faith in their project. And yet exactly this philosophical experiment has been carried out, in full, and has been expanded. This philosophical experiment is the artificial intelligence movement.

What relevance does AI have to theology? Artificial intelligence assumes a particular anthropology, and failures by artificial intelligence may reflect something of interest to theological anthropology. It appears that the artificial intelligence project has failed in a substantial and characteristic way, and furthermore that it has failed as if its assumptions were false—in a way that makes sense given some form of Christian theological anthropology. I will therefore be using the failure of artificial intelligence as a point of departure for the study of theological anthropology. Beyond a negative critique, I will be exploring a positive alternative. The structure of this dissertation will open with critiques, then trace historical development from an interesting alternative to the present problematic state, and then explore that older alternative. I will thus move in the opposite of the usual direction.

For the purposes of this dissertation, *artificial intelligence* (AI) denotes the endeavour to create computer software that will be humanly intelligent, and *cognitive science* the interdisciplinary field which seeks to understand the mind on computational terms so it can be re-implemented on a computer. Artificial intelligence is more focused on programming, whilst cognitive science includes other disciplines such as philosophy of mind, cognitive psychology, and linguistics. *Strong AI* is the classical approach which has generated chess players and theorem provers, and tries to create a disembodied mind. Other areas of artificial intelligence include the *connectionist* school, which works with neural nets,[53] and *embodied AI*,

---

[53] These neural nets are modelled after biological neural nets but are organised differently and seem to take the concept of a neuron on something of a tangent from its organisation and function in a natural brain, be it insect or human.

which tries to take our mind's embodiment seriously. The picture on the cover[54] is from an embodied AI website and is interesting for reasons which I will discuss below under the heading of 'Artificial Intelligence.'

Fraser Watts (2002) and John Puddefoot (1996) offer similar and straightforward pictures of AI. I will depart from them in being less optimistic about the present state of AI, and more willing to find something lurking beneath appearances. I owe my brief remarks about AI and its eschatology, under the heading of 'Artificial Intelligence' below, to a line of Watts' argument.[55]

Other critics[56] argue that artificial intelligence neglects the body as mere packaging for the mind, pointing out ways in which our intelligence is embodied. They share many of the basic assumptions of artificial intelligence but understand our minds as biologically emergent and therefore tied to the body.

There are two basic points I accept in their critiques:

First, they argue that our intelligence is an embodied intelligence, often with specific arguments that are worth attention.

Second, they often capture a quality, or flavour, to thought that beautifully illustrates what sort of thing human thought might be besides digital symbol manipulation on biological hardware.

There are two basic points where I will be departing from their line of argument:

First, they think outside the box, but may not go far enough. They are playing on the opposite team to cognitive

[54] *Cog*, http://www.ai.mit.edu/projects/humanoid-robotics-group/cog/images/cog-rod-slinky.gif, as seen on 11 June 2004 (enlarged).
[55] 2002, 50-1.
[56] Searle 1998, Edelman 1992, etc., including some of Dreyfus 1992. Edelman lists Jerome Brunner, Alan Gauld, Claes von Hofsten, George Lakoff, Ronald Langaker, Ruth Garrett Millikan, Hilary Putnam, John Searle, and Benny Shannon as convergent members of a realist camp (1992, 220).

science researchers, but they are playing the same game, by the same rules. The disagreement between proponents and critics is not whether mind may be explained in purely materialist terms, but only whether that assumption entails that minds can be re-implemented on computers.

Second, they see the mind's ties to the body, but not to the spirit, which means that they miss out on half of a spectrum of interesting critiques. I will seek to explore what, in particular, some of the other half of the spectrum might look like. As their critiques explore what it might mean to say that the mind is embodied, the discussion of reason and intellect under the heading 'Intellect and Reason' below may give some sense of what it might mean to say that the mind is spiritual. In particular, the conception of the intellects offers an interesting base characterisation of human thought that competes with cognitive faculties. Rather than saying that the critics offer false critiques, I suggest that they are too narrow and miss important arguments that are worth exploring.

I will explore failures of artificial intelligence in connection with the Greek Fathers. More specifically, I will look at the seventh century Maximus Confessor's *Mystagogia*. I will investigate the occult as a conduit between the (quasi-Patristic) medieval West and the West today. The use of Orthodox sources could be a particularly helpful light, and one that is not explored elsewhere. Artificial intelligence seems to fail along lines predictable to the patristic understanding of a spirit-soul-body unity, essentially connected with God and other creatures. The discussion becomes more interesting when one looks at the implications of the patristic distinction between 'reason' and the spiritual 'intellect.' I suggest that connections with the Orthodox doctrine of divinisation may make an interesting a direction for future enquiry. I will only make a two-way comparison between Orthodox theological anthropology and one particular quasi-theological anthropology. This dissertation is in particular not an attempt to compare Orthodoxy with other religious traditions.

One wag said that the best book on computer programming for the layperson was *Alice's Adventures in Wonderland*, but that's just because the best book on anything for the layperson was *Alice's Adventures in Wonderland*. One lesson learned by a beginning scholar is that many things that 'everybody knows' are mistaken or half-truths, as 'everybody knows' the truth about Galileo, the Crusades, the Spanish Inquisition, and other select historical topics which we learn about by rumour. There are some things we will have trouble understanding unless we can question what 'everybody knows.' This dissertation will be challenging certain things that 'everybody knows,' such as that we're making progress towards achieving artificial intelligence, that seventh century theology belongs in a separate mental compartment from AI, or that science is a different kind of thing from magic. The result is bound to resemble a tour of Wonderland, not because I am pursuing strangeness for its own sake, but because my attempt to understand artificial intelligence has taken me to strange places. Renaissance and early modern magic is a place artificial intelligence has been, and patristic theology represents what we had to leave to get to artificial intelligence.

The artificial intelligence project as we know it has existed for perhaps half a century, but its roots reach much further back. This picture attests to something that has been a human desire for much longer than we've had digital computers. In exploring the roots of artificial intelligence, there may be reason to look at a topic that may seem strange to mention in connection with science: the Renaissance and early modern occult enterprise.

Why bring the occult into a discussion of artificial intelligence? It doesn't make sense if you accept science's own self-portrayal and look at the past through its eyes. Yet this shows bias and insensitivity to another culture's inner logic, almost a cultural imperialism—not between two cultures today but between the present and the past. A part of what I will be trying to do in this thesis is look at things that have genuine relevance to this question, but whose relevance is obscured by cultural factors today. Our sense of a deep divide between science and magic is more cultural prejudice than considered historical judgment. We judge by the concept of scientific progress, and treating prior cultures' endeavours as more or less successful attempts to establish a scientific enterprise properly measured by our terms.

We miss how the occult turn taken by some of Western culture in the Renaissance and early modern period established lines of development that remain foundational to science today. Many chasms exist between the mediaeval perspective and our own, and there is good reason to place the decisive break between the mediaeval way of life and the Renaissance/early modern occult development, not placing mediaeval times and magic together with an exceptionalism for our science. I suggest that our main differences with the occult project are disagreements as to means, not ends—and that distinguishes the post-mediaeval West from the mediaevals. If so, there is a kinship between the occult project and our own time: we provide a variant answer to the same question as the Renaissance magus, whilst patristic and mediaeval Christians were exploring another question altogether. The occult vision has fragmented, with its dominion over the natural world becoming scientific technology, its vision for a better world becoming political ideology, and its spiritual practices becoming a private fantasy.

One way to look at historical data in a way that shows the kind of sensitivity I'm interested in, is explored by Mary Midgley in *Science as Salvation* (1992); she doesn't dwell on the occult as such, but she perceptively argues that science is far more continuous with religion than its self-understanding would suggest. Her approach pays a certain kind of attention to things which science leads us to ignore. She looks at ways science is doing far more than falsifying hypotheses, and in so doing observes some things which are important. I hope to develop a similar argument in a different direction, arguing that science is far more continuous with the occult than its self-understanding would suggest. This thesis is intended neither to be a correction nor a refinement of her position, but development of a parallel line of enquiry.

It is as if a great island, called Magic, began to drift away from the cultural mainland. It had plans for what the mainland should be converted into, but had no wish to be associated with the mainland. As time passed, the island fragmented into smaller islands, and on all of these new islands the features hardened and became more sharply defined. One of the islands is named Ideology. The one we are interested in is Science, which is not interchangeable with the original Magic, but is even less independent: in some ways Science differs from Magic by being more like Magic than Magic itself. Science is further from the mainland than Magic was, even if its influence on the mainland is if anything greater than what Magic once held. I am interested in a scientific endeavour, and in particular a basic relationship behind scientific enquiry, which are to a substantial degree continuous with a magical endeavour and a basic relationship behind magic. These are foundationally important, and even if it is not yet clear what they may mean, I will try to substantiate these as the thesis develops. I propose the idea of Magic breaking off from a societal mainland, and sharpening and hardening into Science, as more helpful than the idea of science and magic as opposites.

There is in fact historical precedent for such a phenomenon. I suggest that a parallel with Eucharistic doctrine might illuminate the interrelationship between Orthodoxy, Renaissance and early modern magic, and science (including artificial intelligence). When Aquinas

made the Christian-Aristotelian synthesis, he changed the
doctrine of the Eucharist. The Eucharist had previously
been understood on Orthodox terms that used a Platonic
conception of bread and wine participating in the body and
blood of Christ, so that bread remained bread whilst
becoming the body of Christ. One substance had two
natures. Aristotelian philosophy had little room for one
substance which had two natures, so one thing cannot
simultaneously be bread and the body of Christ. When
Aquinas subsumed real presence doctrine under an
Aristotelian framework, he managed a delicate balancing
act, in which bread ceased to be bread when it became the
body of Christ, and it was a miracle that the accidents of
bread held together after the substance had changed. I
suggest that when Zwingli expunged real presence doctrine
completely, he was not abolishing the Aristotelian impulse,
but carrying it to its proper end. In like fashion, the
scientific movement is not a repudiation of the magical
impulse, but a development of it according to its own inner
logic. It expunges the supernatural as Zwingli expunged the
real presence, because that is where one gravitates once the
journey has begun. What Aquinas and the Renaissance
magus had was composed of things that did not fit together.
As I will explore below under the heading 'Renaissance and
Early Modern Magic,' the Renaissance magus ceased
relating to society as to one's mother and began treating it
as raw material; this foundational change to a
depersonalised relationship would later secularise the
occult and transform it into science. The parallel between
medieval Christianity/magic/science and
Orthodoxy/Aquinas/Zwingli seems to be fertile: real
presence doctrine can be placed under an Aristotelian
framework, and a sense of the supernatural can be held by
someone who is stepping out of a personal kind of
relationship, but in both cases it doesn't sit well, and after
two or so centuries people finished the job by subtracting
the supernatural.

Without discussing the principles in Thomas Dixon's 1999 delineation of theology, anti-theology, and atheology that can be un-theological or quasi-theological, regarding when one is justified in claiming that theology is present, I adopt the following rule:

A claim is considered *quasi-theological* if it can conflict with theological claims.

Given this rule, patristic theology, Renaissance and early modern magic (hereafter 'magic' or 'the occult'), and artificial intelligence claims are all considered to be theological or quasi-theological.

I will not properly trace an historical development so much as show the distinctions between archetypal scientific, occult, and Orthodox worldviews as seen at different times, and briefly discuss their relationships with some historical remarks. Not only are there surprisingly persistent tendencies, but Lee repeats Weber's suggestion that there is real value to understand ideal types.[57]

I will be attempting to bring together pieces of a puzzle—pieces scattered across disciplines and across centuries, often hidden by today's cultural assumptions about what is and is not connected—to show their interconnections and the picture that emerges from their fit. I will be looking at features including intentionality,[58] teleology,[59] cognitive faculties,[60] the spiritual intellect,[61]

---

[57] Lee 1987, 6.
[58] 'Intentionality' is a philosophy of mind term for the 'about-ness' of mental states.
[59] By 'teleology' I understand in a somewhat inclusive sense that branch of theology and philosophy that deals with goals, ends, and ultimate meanings.
[60] By 'teleology' I understand in a somewhat inclusive sense that branch of theology and philosophy that deals with goals, ends, and ultimate meanings.
[61] The spiritual 'intellect' is a patristic concept that embraces thought, conceived on different terms from 'cognitive science,' and is

cosmology, and a strange figure who wields a magic sword with which to slice through society's Gordian knots. Why? In a word, all of this connected. Cosmology is relevant if there is a cosmological error behind artificial intelligence. There are both an organic connection and a distinction between teleology and intentionality, and the shift from teleology to intentionality is an important shift; when one shifts from teleology to intentionality one becomes partly blind to what the artificial intelligence picture is missing. Someone brought up on cognitive faculties may have trouble answering, 'How else could it be?'; the patristic understanding of the spiritual intellect gives a very interesting answer, and offers a completely different way to understand thought. And the figure with the magic sword? I'll let this figure remain mysterious for the moment, but I'll hint that without that metaphorical magic sword we would never have a literal artificial intelligence project. I do not believe I am forging new connections among these things, so much as uncovering something that was already there, overlooked but worth investigating.

       This is an attempt to connect some very diverse sources, even if the different sections are meant primarily as philosophy of religion. This brings problems of coherence and disciplinary consistency, but the greater risk is tied to the possibility of greater reward. It will take more work to show connections than in a more externally focused enquiry, but if I can give a believable case for those interconnections, this will *ipso facto* be a more interesting enquiry.

       All translations from French, German, Latin, and Greek are my own.

---

inseparably the place where a person meets God. Augustine locates the image of God in the intellect (*In Euangelium Ioannis Tractatus*, III.4), and compares the intellect to Christ as illuminating both itself and everything else (*In Euangelium Ioannis Tractatus*, XLVII, 3).

Artificial Intelligence

Artificial intelligence is not just one scientific project among others. It is a cultural manifestation of a timeless dream. It does not represent the repudiation of the occult impulse, but letting that impulse work out according to its own inner logic. Artificial intelligence is connected with a transhumanist vision for the future[62] which tries to create a science-fiction-like future of an engineered society of superior beings.[63] This artificial intelligence vision for the future is similar to the occult visions for the future we will see below. Very few members of the artificial intelligence movement embrace the full vision—but I may suggest that its spectre is rarely absent, and that that spectre shows itself by a perennial sense of, 'We're making real breakthroughs today, and full AI is just around the corner.' Both those who embrace the fuller enthusiasm and those who are more modestly excited by current project have a hope that we are making progress towards creating something fundamentally new under the sun, of bequeathing humanity with something that has never before been available, machines that genuinely think. Indeed, this kind of hope is one of magic's most salient features. The exact content and features vary, but the sometimes heady excitement and the hope to bestow something powerful and new mark a significant point contact between the artificial intelligence and the magic that enshrouded science's birth.

There is something timeless and archetypal about the desire to create humans through artifice instead of procreation. Jewish legend tells of a rabbi who used the

[62] Watts 2002, 57-8. See the World Transhumanist Association website at http://www.transhumanist.org for further information on transhumanism.
[63] C.S. Lewis critiques this project in *The Abolition of Man* (1943) and *That Hideous Strength* (1965). He does not address the question of whether this is a possible goal, but argues that it is not a desirable goal: the glorious future it heralds is in fact a horror compared to the present it so disparages.

Kaballah to create a clay golem to defend a city against anti-
semites in 1581.[64] *Frankenstein* has so marked the popular
imagination that genetically modified foods are referred to
as 'Frankenfoods,' and there are many (fictional) stories of
scientists creating androids who rebel against and possibly
destroy their creators. Robots who have artificial bodies but
think and act enough like humans never to cause culture
shock are a staple of science fiction.[65] There is a timeless
and archetypal desire to create humans by artifice rather
than procreation. Indeed, this desire has more than a little
occult resonance.

   We should draw a distinction between what may be
called 'pretentious AI' and 'un-pretentious AI.' The artificial
intelligence project has managed technical feats that are
sometimes staggering, and from a computer scientist's
perspective, the state of computer science is richer and
more mature than if there had been no artificial intelligence
project. Without making any general claim that artificial
intelligence achieves nothing or achieves nothing
significant, I will explore a more specific and weaker claim
that artificial intelligence does not and cannot duplicate
human intelligence.

   A paradigm example of un-pretentious AI is the
United States Postal Service handwriting recognition
system. It succeeds in reading the addresses on 85% of
postal items, and the USPS annual report is justifiably
proud of this achievement.[66] However, there is nothing
mythic claimed for it: the USPS does not claim a major
breakthrough in emulating human thought, nor does it give

[64] *Encyclopedia Mythica*, 'Rabbi Loeb,'
   http://www.pantheon.org/articles/r/rabbi_loeb.html, as seen on
   26 Mar 04.
[65] Foerst 1998, 109 also brings up this archetypal tendency in her
   conclusion.
[66] United States Postal Service 2003 annual report,
   http://www.usps.com/history/anrpto3/html/realkind.htm, as
   seen on 6 May 2004.

people the impression that artificial mail carriers are just around the corner. The handwriting recognition system is a tool—admittedly, quite an impressive tool—but it is nothing more than a tool, and no one pretends it is anything more than a tool.

For a paradigm example of pretentious AI, I will look at something different. The robot Cog represents equally impressive feats in artificial hand-eye coordination and motor control, but its creators claim something deeper, something archetypal and mythic:

Fig. 2: Cog, portrayed as Robo sapiens[67]

The scholar places his hand on the robots' shoulder as if they had a longstanding friendship. At almost every semiotic level, this picture constitutes an implicit claim that the researcher has a deep friendship with what must be a deep being. The unfortunately blurred caption reads, '©2000 Peter Menzel / Robo sapiens.' On the Cog main website area, every picture with Cog and a person

[67] *Cog*, as seen on http://www.ai.mit.edu/projects/humanoid-robotics-group/cog/images/scaz-cog.gif, on 6 May 2004 (enlarged).

theatrically shows the person treating the robot as quite lifelike—giving the impression that the robot must be essentially human.

But how close is Cog to being human? Watts writes,

> The weakness of Cog at present seems to be that it cannot actually do very much. Even its insect-like computer forebears do not seem to have had the intelligence of insects, and Cog is clearly nowhere near having human intelligence.[68]

The somewhat light-hearted frequently-asked-questions list acknowledges that the robot 'has no idea what it did two minutes ago,' answers 'Can Cog pass the Turing test?' by saying, 'No... but neither could an infant,' and interestingly answers 'Is Cog conscious?' by saying, 'We try to avoid using the c-word in our lab. For the record, no. Off the record, we have no idea what that question even means. And still, no.' The response to a very basic question is ambiguous, but it seems to joke that 'consciousness' is obscene language, and gives the impression that this is not an appropriate question to ask: a mature adult, when evaluating our AI, does not childishly frame the question in terms of consciousness. Apparently, we should accept the optimistic impression of Cog, whilst recognising that it's not fair to the robot to ask about features of human personhood that the robot can't exhibit. This smells of begging the question.

Un-pretentious AI makes an impressive technical achievement, but recognises and acknowledges that they've created a tool and not something virtually human. Pretentious AI can make equally impressive technical achievements, and it recognises that what it's created is not equivalent to human, but it does not acknowledge this. The

---

[68] 2002, 57.

answer to 'Is Cog conscious?' is a refusal to acknowledge something the researchers have to recognise: that Cog has no analogue to human consciousness. Is it a light-hearted way of making a serious claim of strong agnosticism about Cog's consciousness? It doesn't read much like a mature statement that 'We could never know if Cog were conscious.' The researcher in Figure 2 wrote an abstract on how to give robots a theory of other minds,[69] which reads more like psychology than computer science.

There's something going on here that also goes on in the occult. In neo-paganism, practitioners find their magic to work, not exactly as an outsider would expect, by making incantations and hoping that something will happen that a skeptic would recognise as supernatural, but by doing what they can and then interpreting reality as if the magic had worked. They create an illusion and subconsciously embrace it. This mechanism works well enough, in fact, that large segments of today's neo-paganism started as jokes and then became real, something their practitioners took quite seriously.[70] There's power in trying to place a magical incantation or a computer program (or, in programmer slang, 'incantation') to fill a transcendent hope: one finds ways that it appears to work, regardless of what an outsider's interpretation may be. This basic technique appears to be at work in magic as early as the Renaissance, and it appears to be exactly what's going on in pretentious AI. The basic factor of stepping into an illusion after you do what you can makes sense of the rhetoric quoted above and why Cog is portrayed not merely as a successful experiment in coordination but as Robo sapiens, the successful creation of a living golem. Of course we don't interpret it as magic because we assume that artificial and intelligence and magic

[69] *Cog*, 'Theory of Mind for a Humanoid Robots,' http://www.ai.mit.edu/projects/humanoid-robotics/group/cog/Abstracts2000/scaz.pdf, as seen on 6 May 2004.
[70] Adler 1986, 319-321.

are very different things, but the researchers' self-deception falls into a quite venerable magical tradition.

Computers seem quite logical. Are they really that far from human rationality? Computers are logical without being rational. Programming a computer is like explaining a task to someone who follows directions very well but has no judgment and no ability to recognise broader intentions in a request. It follows a list of instructions without any recognition or a sense of what is being attempted. The ability to understand a conversation, or recognise another person's intent—even with mistakes—or any of a number of things humans take for granted, belongs to rationality. A computer's behaviour is built up from logical rules that do certain precise manipulations of symbols without any sense of meaning whatsoever: it is logical without being rational. The discipline of usability is about how to write well-designed computer programs; these programs usually let the user forget that computers aren't rational. For instance, a user can undo something when the computer logically and literally follows an instruction, and the user rationally realises that that isn't really what was intended. But even the best of this design doesn't let the computer understand what one meant to say. One frustration people have with computers stems from the fact that there is a gist to what humans say, and other people pick up that gist. Computers do not have even the most rudimentary sense of gist, only the ability to logically follow instructions. This means that the experience of bugs and debugging in programming is extremely frustrating to those learning how to program; the computer's response to what seems a correct program goes beyond nitpicking. This logicality without rationality is deceptive, for it presents something that looks very much like rationality at first glance, but produces unpleasant surprises when you treat it as rational. There's something interesting going on here. When we read rationality into a computer's logicality, we are in part creating the illusion of artificial intelligence. 'Don't anthropomorphise computers,' one tells novice programmers. 'They hate that.' A computer is logical enough that we tend to treat it as rational, and in fact if you want to believe that you've achieved artificial intelligence, you have an excellent basis to use in forming a magician's self-deception.

Artificial intelligence is a mythic attempt to create an artificial person, and it does so in a revealing way. Thought is assumed to be a private manipulation of mental representations, not something that works in terms of spirit. Embodied AI excluded, the body is assumed to be packaging, and the attempt is not just to duplicate the 'mind' in a complete sense, but our more computer-like rationality: this assumes a highly significant division of what is essential, what is packaging, and what comes along for free if you duplicate the essential bits. None of this is simply how humans have always thought, nor is it neutral. Maximus Confessor's assumptions are different enough from AI's that a comparison makes it easier to see some of AI's assumptions, and furthermore what sort of coherent picture could deny them. I will explore how exactly he does so below under the heading 'Orthodox Anthropology in Maximus Confessor's *Mystagogia*,' More immediately, I wish to discuss a basic type of assumption shared by artificial intelligence and the occult.

The Optimality Assumption

One commonality that much of magic and science share is that broad visions often include the assumption that what they don't understand must be simple, and be easy to modify or improve. Midgley discusses Bernal's exceedingly optimistic hope for society to transform itself into a simplistically conceived scientific Utopia (if perhaps lacking most of what we value in human society);[71] I will discuss later, under various headings, how society simply

[71] Adler 1986, 319-321.

works better in Thomas More's and B.F. Skinner's Utopias if only it is re-engineered according to their simple models.[72] Aren't Utopian visions satires, not prescriptions? I would argue that the satire itself has a strong prescriptive element, even if it's not literal. The connection between Utopia and AI is that the same sort of thinking feeds into what, exactly, is needed to duplicate a human mind. For instance, let us examine a sample of dialogue which Turing imagined going on in a Turing test:

> Q: Please write me a sonnet on the subject of the Forth Bridge.
>
> A: Count me out on this one. I never could write poetry.
>
> Q: Add 34957 to 70764.
>
> A: (Pause about 30 seconds and then give as answer) 105621.
>
> Q: Do you play chess?
>
> A: Yes.
>
> Q: I have K at my K1, and no other pieces. You have only K at K6 and R at R1. It is your move. What do you play?
>
> A: (After a pause of 15 seconds) R-R8 mate.[73]

Turing seems to assume that if you duplicate his favoured tasks of arithmetic and chess, the task of understanding natural language comes along, more or less

[72] Utopias are often a satire more than a prescription literally conceived, but they are also far more prescriptive than one would gather from a simple statement that they are satire.
[73] Turing 1950.

for free. The subsequent history of artificial intelligence has not been kind to this assumption. Setting aside the fact that most people do not strike up a conversation by strangely requesting the other person to solve a chess problem and add five-digit numbers, Turing is showing an occult way of thinking by assuming there's nothing really obscure, or deep, about the human person, and that the range of cognitive tasks needed to do AI is the range of tasks that immediately present themselves to him. This optimism may be damped by subsequent setbacks which the artificial intelligence movement has experienced, but it's still present. It's hard to see an artificial intelligence researcher saying, 'The obvious problem looks hard to solve, but there are probably hidden problems which are much harder,' let alone consider whether human thought might be non-computational.

Given the difficulties they acknowledge, artificial intelligence researchers seem to assume that the problem is as easy as possible to solve. As I will discuss later, this kind of assumption has profound occult resonance. I will call this assumption the optimality assumption: with allowances and caveats, the optimality assumption states that artificial intelligence is an optimally easy problem to solve. This doesn't mean an optimally easy problem to solve given the easiest possible world, but rather, taking into the difficulties and nuances recognised by the practitioner, the problem is then assumed to be optimally easy, and then it could be said that we live in the (believable) possible world where artificial intelligence would be easiest to implement. Anything that doesn't work like a computer is assumedly easy, or a matter of unnecessary packaging. There are variations on the theme of begging the question. One basic strategy of ensuring that computers can reach the bar of human intelligence is to lower the bar until it is already met. Another strategy is to try to duplicate human intelligence on computer-like tasks. Remember the Turing test which Turing imagined, which seemed to recognise only the cognitive tasks of writing a poem, doing arithmetic, and solving a chess problem: Turing apparently assumed that natural language understanding would come along for free by the time computers could do both arithmetic and chess. Now we have computer calculators and chess players that can beat humans, whilst natural language understanding tasks which are simple to humans represent an unscaled Everest to artificial intelligence.

We have a situation very much like the attempt to make a robot that can imitate human locomotion—if the attempt is tested by having a robot race a human athlete on a racetrack ergonomically designed for robots. Chess is about as computer-like a human skill as one could find.

Turing's script for an imagined Turing test is one manifestation of a tendency to assume that the problem is optimally easy: the optimality assumption. Furthermore, Turing sees only three tasks of composing a sonnet, adding two numbers, and making a move in chess. But in fact this leaves out a task of almost unassailable difficulty for AI: understanding and appropriately acting on natural language requests. This is part of human rationality that cannot simply be assumed to come with a computer's logicality.

Four decades after Turing imagined the above dialogue, Kurt VanLehn describes a study of problem solving that used a standard story problem.[74] The ensuing discussion is telling. Two subjects' interpretations are treated as problems to be resolved, apparently chosen for their departure from how a human 'should' think about these things. One is a nine year old girl, Cathy: '...It is apparent from [her] protocol that Cathy solves this problem by imagining the physical situation and the actions taken in it, as opposed to, say, converting the puzzle to a directed graph then finding a traversal of the graph.' The purpose of the experiment was to understand how humans solve

[74] VanLehn 1989, in Posner 1989, 532.

problems, but it was approached with a tunnel vision that gave a classic kind of computer science 'graph theory' problem, wrapped up in words, and treated any other interpretation of those words as an interesting abnormality. It seems that it is not the theory's duty to approach the subject matter, but the subject matter's duty to approach the theory—a signature trait of occult projects. Is this merely VanLehn's tunnel vision? He goes on to describe the state of cognitive science itself:

> For instance, one can ask a subject to draw a pretty picture... [such] Problems whose understanding is not readily represented as a problem space are called *ill-defined*. Sketching pretty pictures is an example of an ill-defined problem... There have only been a few studies of ill-defined problem solving.[75]

Foerst summarises a tradition of feminist critique:[76] AI was started by men who chose a particular kind of abstract task as the hallmark of intelligence; women might value disembodied abstraction less and might choose something like social skills. The critique may be pushed one step further than that: beyond any claim that AI researchers, when looking for a basis for computer intelligence, tacitly crystallised intelligence out of men's activities rather than women's, it seems that their minds were so steeped in mathematics and computers that they crystallised intelligence out of human performance more in computer-like activities than anything essentially human, even in a masculine way. Turing didn't talk about making artificial car mechanics or deer hunters any more than he had plans for artificial hostesses or childminders.

[75] *Ibid.* in Posner 1989, 534.
[76] 1998, 101.

Harman's 1989 account of functionalism, for instance, provides a more polished-looking version of an optimality assumption: 'According to functionalism, it does not matter what mental states and processes are made of any more than it matters what a carburetor or heart or a chess king is made of.' (832). Another suggestion may be made, not as an axiom but as an answer to the question, 'How else could it be?' This other suggestion might be called *the tip of the iceberg conception.*

A 'tip of the iceberg' conception might reply, 'Suppose for the sake of argument that it doesn't matter what an iceberg is made of, so long as it sticks up above the surface and is hard enough to sink a ship. The task is then to make an artificial iceberg. One can hire engineers to construct a hard shell to function as a surrogate iceberg. What has been left out is that these properties of something observable from the surface rest on something that lies much, much deeper than the surface. (A mere scrape with an iceberg sunk the Titanic, not only because the iceberg was hard, but because it had an iceberg's monumental inertia behind that hardness.) One can't make a functional tip of the iceberg that way, because a functional tip of an iceberg requires a functional iceberg, and we have very little idea of how to duplicate those parts of an iceberg that aren't visible from a ship. You are merely assuming that one can try hard enough to duplicate what you can see from a ship, and if you duplicate those observables, everything else will follow.' This is not a fatal objection, but it is intended to suggest what the truth could be besides the repeated assumption that intelligence is as easy as possible to duplicate in a computer. Here again is the optimality assumption, and it is a specific example of a broader optimality assumption which will appear in occult sources discussed under the 'Renaissance and Early Modern Magic' heading below. The 'tip of the iceberg' conception is notoriously absent in occult and artificial intelligence sources alike. In occult sources, the endeavour is to create a magically sharp sword that will slice all of the Gordian knots of society's problems; in artificial intelligence the Gordian knots are not societal problems but obstacles to creating a thinking machine, and researchers may only be attempting to use razor blades to cut tangled shoelaces, but researchers are still trying to get as close to that magic sword as they believe possible.

Just Around the Corner Since 1950

The artificial intelligence movement has a number of reasonably stable features, including an abiding sense of 'Today's discoveries are a real breakthrough; artificial minds are just around the corner.' This mood may even be older than digital computers; Dreyfus writes,

> In the period between the invention of the telephone relay and its apotheosis in the digital computer, the brain, always understood in terms of the latest technological inventions, was understood as a large telephone switchboard, or more recently, as an electronic computer.[77]

The discoveries and the details of the claim may change, and experience has battered some of strong AI's optimism, but in pioneers and today's embodied AI advocates alike there is a similar mood: 'What we've developed now is effacing the boundary between machine and human.' This mood is quite stable. There is a striking similarity between the statements,

> These emotions [discomfort and shock at something so human-like] might arise because

[77] 1992, 159.

in our interactions with Cog, little
distinguishes us from the robot, and the
differences between a machine and its human
counterparts fade.[78]

and:

The reader must accept it as a fact that digital
computers can be constructed, and indeed
have been constructed, according to the
principles we have described, and that they
can in fact mimic the actions of a human
computer very closely.[79]

What is interesting here is that the second was made
by Turing in 1950, and the first by Foerst in 1998. As
regards Turing, no one now believes 1950 computers could
perform any but the most menial of mathematicians' tasks,
and some of Cog's weaknesses have been discussed above
("Cog... cannot actually do very much. Even its insect-like
forebears do not seem to have had the intelligence of
insects..."). The more artificial intelligence changes, the
more it seems to stay the same. The overall impression one
receives is that for all the surface progress of the artificial
intelligence, the underlying philosophy and spirit remain
the same—and part of this underlying spirit is the
conviction, 'We're making real breakthroughs now, and full
artificial intelligence is just around the corner.' This self-
deception is sustained in classically magical fashion.
Artificial intelligence's self-presentation exudes novelty, a
sense that today's breakthroughs are decisive—whilst its
actual rate of change is much slower. The 'It's just around
the corner.' rhetoric is a longstanding feature. For all the
changes in processor power and greater consistency in a

[78] Foerst 1998, 103.
[79] Turing 1950.

materialist doctrine of mind, there are salient features which seem to repeat in 1950's and today's cognitive science. In both, the strategy to ensure that computers could jump the bar of human intelligence is by lowering the bar until it had already been jumped.

The Ghost in the Machine

It has been suggested in connection with Polanyi's understanding of tacit knowledge that behaviourists did not teach, 'There is no soul.' Rather, they draw students into a mode of enquiry where the possibility of a soul is never considered.

> Modern psychology takes completely for granted that behavior and neural function are perfectly correlated, that one is completely caused by the other. There is no separate soul or lifeforce to stick a finger into the brain now and then and make neural cells do what they would not otherwise. Actually, of course, this is a working assumption only....It is quite conceivable that someday the assumption will have to be rejected. But it is important also to see that we have not reached that day yet: the working assumption is a necessary one and there is no real evidence opposed to it. Our failure to solve a problem so far does not make it insoluble. One cannot logically be a determinist in physics and biology, and a mystic in psychology.[80]

This is a balder and more provocative way of stating what writers like Turing lead the reader to never think of questioning. The assumption is that the soul, if there is one,

[80] Hebb 1949, as quoted in the Linux 'fortune' program.

is by nature external and separate from the body, so that any interaction between the two is a violation of the body's usual way of functioning. Thus what is denied is a 'separate soul or lifeforce to stick a finger into the brain now and then and make neural cells do what they would not do otherwise.' The Orthodox and others' doctrine of unified personhood is very different from an affirmation of a ghost in the machine. To affirm a ghost in the machine is to assume the soul's basic externality to the body: the basic inability of a soul to interact with a body creates the problem of the ghost in the machine. By the time one attempts to solve the problem of the ghost in the machine, one is already outside of an Orthodox doctrine of personhood in which spirit, soul, and body are united and the whole unit is not an atom.

The objective here is not mainly to criticise AI, but to see what can be learned: AI seems to fail in a way that is characteristic. It does not fail because of insufficient funding or lack of technical progress, but on another plane: it is built on an erroneous quasi-theological anthropology, and its failures may suggest something about being human. The main goal is to answer the question, 'How else could it be?' in a way that is missed by critics working in materialist confines.

What can we say in summary?

First, artificial intelligence work may be divided into un-pretentious and pretentious AI. Un-pretentious AI makes tools that no one presents as anything more than tools. Pretentious AI is presented as more human than is properly warranted.

Second, there are stable features to the artificial intelligence movement, including a claim of, 'We have something essentially human. With today's discoveries, full artificial intelligence is just around the corner.' The exact form of this assertion may change, but the basic claim does not.

Third, artificial intelligence research posits a multifarious 'optimality assumption,' namely that, given the caveats recognised by the researcher, artificial intelligence is an optimally easy assumption to solve. The human mind is assumed to be the sort of thing that is optimally easy to re-create on a computer.

Fourth, artificial intelligence comes from the same kind of thinking as the ghost in the machine problem.

There is more going on in the artificial intelligence project than an attempt to produce scientific results. The persistent rhetoric of 'It's just around the corner,' is not because artificial intelligence scientists have held that sober judgment since the project began, but because there's something else going on. For reasons that I hope will become clearer in the next section, this is beginning to look like an occult project—a secularised occult project, perhaps, but 'secularised occult' is not an empty term in that you take all of the occult away if you take away spellbooks. There is much more to the occult than crystal balls, and a good deal of this 'much more' is at play even if artificial intelligence doesn't do things the *Skeptical Enquirer* would frown on.

Occult Foundations of Modern Science

With acknowledgment of the relevance of the Reformation, the wake of Aristotelianism, and the *via moderna* of nominalism,[81] I will be looking at a surprising candidate for discussion on this topic: magic. Magic was a large part of what shaped modernity, a much larger factor than one would expect from modernity's own self-portrayal, and it has been neglected for reasons besides than the disinterested pursuit of truth. It is more attractive to our

---

[81] Nominalism said that general categories are something in the mind drawn from real things, and not something things themselves arise from. This has profoundly shaped the course of Western culture.

culture to say that our science exists in the wake of
Renaissance learning or brave Reformers than to say that
science has roots in it decries as superstition. For reasons
that I will discuss below under the next heading, I suggest
that what we now classify as the artificial intelligence
movement is a further development of some of magic's
major features.

There is a major qualitative shift between Newton's
development of physics being considered by some to be a
diversion from his alchemical and other occult endeavours,
and 'spooky' topics today being taboo for scientific research.
Yet it is still incomplete to enter a serious philosophical
discussion of science without understanding the occult, as
as it incomplete to enter a serious discussion of Christianity
without understanding Judaism. Lewis points out that the
popular understanding of modern science displacing the
magic of the middle ages is at least misleading; there was
very little magic in the middle ages, and then science and
magic flourished at the same time, for the same reason,
often in the same people: the reason science became
stronger than magic is purely Darwinian: it worked better.[82]
One may say that medieval religion is the matrix from
which Renaissance magic departed, and early modern
magic is the matrix from which science departed.

What is the relationship between the mediaeval West
and patristic Christianity? In this context, the practical
difference is not yet a great one. The essential difference is
that certain seeds have been sown—such as nominalism and
the rediscovered Aristotelianism—which in the mediaeval
West would grow into something significant, but had not in
much of any practical sense affected the fabric of society.
People still believed that the heavens told the glory of God;
people lived a life oriented towards contemplation rather
than consumption; monasteries and saints were assumed so
strongly that they were present even—especially—as they

[82] Lewis 1943, 46.

retreated from society. Certain seeds had been sown in the mediaeval West, but they had not grown to any significant stature. For this discussion, I will treat mediaeval and patristic Christianity as more alike than different.

Renaissance and Early Modern Magic

Magic in this context is much more than a means of casting spells or otherwise manipulating supernatural powers to obtain results. That practice is the token of an entire worldview and enterprise, something that defines life's meaning and what one ought to seek. To illustrate this, I will look at some details of work by a characteristic figure, Leibniz. Then I will look at the distinctive way the Renaissance magus related to the world and the legacy this relationship has today. Alongside this I will look at a shift from understanding this life as a contemplative apprenticeship to Heaven, to understanding this life as something for us to make more pleasurable.

Leibniz, a 17th century mathematician and scientist who co-discovered calculus, appears to have been more than conversant with the occult memory tradition,[83] and his understanding of calculus was not, as today, a tool used by engineers to calculate volumes. Rather, it was part of an entire Utopian vision, which could encompass all knowledge and all thoughts, an apparently transcendent tool that would obviate the need for philosophical disagreements:

> If we had this [calculus], there would be no
> more reason for disputes between
> philosophers than between accountants. It
> would be enough for them to take their quills
> and say, 'Let us calculate!'

[83] Yates 1966, 380-382.

Leibniz's 1690 *Ars Combinatoria* contains some material that is immediately accessible to a modern mathematician. It also contains material that is less accessible. Much of the second chapter (9-48) discusses combinations of the letters U, P, J, S, A, and N; these letters are tied to concepts ranging from philosophy to theology, jurisprudence and mathematics: another table links philosophical concepts with numbers (42-3). The apparent goal was to validly manipulate concepts through mechanical manipulations of words, but I was unable to readily tell what (mathematico-logical?) principle was supposed to make this work. (The principle is apparently unfamiliar to me.) This may reflect the influence of Ramon Lull, thirteenth century magician and doctor of the Catholic Church who adapted a baptised Kaballah which involved manipulating combinations of (Latin) letters. Leibniz makes repeated reference to Lull (28, 31, 34, 46), and specifically mentions his occult *ars magna* (28). Like Lull, Leibniz is interested in the occult, and seeks to pioneer some new tool that will obviate the need for this world's troubles. He was an important figure in the creation of science, and his notation is still used for calculus today. Leibniz is not trying to be just another member of society, or to contribute to society's good the way members have always contributed to society's good: he stands above it, and his intended contribution is to reorder the fabric of society according to his endowed vision. Leibniz provides a characteristic glimpse of how early modern magic has left a lasting imprint.

If the person one should be in Orthodoxy is the member of Church and society, the figure in magic is the magus, a singular character who stands outside of the fabric of society and seeks to transform it. What is the difference? The member of the faithful is an integrated part of society, and lives in submission and organic connection to it. The magus, by contrast, stands above society, superior to it, having a relation to society as one whose right and perhaps duty is to tear apart and reconstruct society along better lines. We have a difference between humility and pride, between relating to society as to one's mother and treating society as raw material for one to transform. The magus is cut off from the common herd by two closely related endowments: a magic sword to cut through society's Gordian knots, and a messianic fantasy.[84] In Leibniz's case the magic sword is an artificial language which will make philosophical disagreements simply obsolete. For the artificial intelligence movement, the magic sword is artificial intelligence itself. The exact character of the sword, knot, and fantasy may differ, but their presence does not.

The character of the Renaissance magus may be seen as as hinging on despair with the natural world. This mood seems to be woven into Hermetic texts that were held in such esteem in the Renaissance and were connected at the opening of pre-eminent Renaissance neo-Platonist Pico della Mirandola's *Oration on the Dignity of Man*.[85] If there is good to be had, it is not met in the mundane world of the *hoi polloi*. It must be very different from their reality, something hidden that is only accessible to an elite. The sense in which this spells out an interest in the occult means far more than carrying around a rabbit's foot. The specific supernatural contact was valued because the occult was far hidden from appearances and the unwashed masses. (The Christian claim that one can simply pray to God and be heard is thus profoundly uninteresting. Supernatural as it may be, it is ordinary, humble, and accessible in a way that

[84] Without submitting to the Church in the usual way, the magus is equal to its highest members (Webster 1982, 57).
[85] George Mason University's *Modern & Classical Languages*, 'Pico della Mirandola: Oratio de hominis dignitate,' http://www.gmu.edu/departments/fld/CLASSICS/mirandola.orati o.html, as seen on 18 May 2004. See Poim 27-9, CH7 1-2 in Bentley 1987 for texts reflecting an understanding of the world as evil and associated contempt for the *hoi polloi*.

the magus is trying to push past.) This desire for what is hidden or very different from the ordinary means that the ideal future must be very different from the present. Therefore Thomas More, Renaissance author, canonised saint, and strong devotee of Mirandola's writing, himself writes *Utopia*. In this work, the philosophic sailor Raphael establishes his own reason as judge over the appropriateness of executing thieves,[86] and describes a Utopia where society simply works better: there seem to be no unpleasant surprises or unintended consequences.[87] There is little sense of a complex inner logic to society that needs to be respected, or any kind of authority to submit to. Indeed, Raphael abhors authority and responds to the suggestion that he attach himself to a king's court by saying, 'Happier! Is that to follow a path that my soul abhors?' This Utopian vision, even if it is from a canonised Roman saint, captures something deep of the occult currents that would later feed into the development of political ideology. The content of an occult vision for constructing a better tomorrow may vary, but it is a vision that seeks to tear up the world as we now know it and reconstructs it along different lines.

Magic and science alike relate to what they are interested in via an I-It rather than an I-Thou relationship. Relating to society as to one's mother is an I-Thou

---

[86] *Thomas More: Utopia, Digitale Rekonstruktion*, http://www.ub.uni-bielefeld.de/cgi-bin/button.cgi?pfad=/diglib/more/utopia/jpeg/&seite=00000017.jpg&jump=1, http://www.ub.uni-bielefeld.de/cgi-bin/button.cgi?pfad=/diglib/more/utopia/jpeg/&seite=00000018.jpg&jump=1, etc. (pp. 35-6), as seen on 2 June 2004.

[87] *Thomas More: Utopia, Digitale Rekonstruktion*, http://www.ub.uni-bielefeld.de/cgi-bin/button.cgi?pfad=/diglib/more/utopia/jpeg/&seite=00000039.jpg&jump=1, http://www.ub.uni-bielefeld.de/cgi-bin/button.cgi?pfad=/diglib/more/utopia/jpeg/&seite=00000040.jpg&jump=1, etc., (pp. 79-86), as seen on 2 June 2004. This runs through most of the book.

relationship; treating society as raw material is an I-It relationship. An I-Thou relationship is receptive to quality. It can gain wisdom and insight. It can connect out of the whole person. The particular kind of I-It relationship that undergirds science has a powerful and narrow tool that deals in what can be mathematically represented. The difference between those two is misunderstood if one stops after saying, 'I-It can make technology available much better than I-Thou.' That is how things look through I-It eyes. But I-Thou allows a quality of relationship that does not exist with I-It. 'The fundamental word I-Thou can only be spoken with one's whole being. The fundamental word I-It can never be spoken with one's whole being.' I-Thou allows a quality-rich relationship that always has another layer of meaning. In the Romance languages there are two different words for knowledge: in French, *connaissance* and *savoir*. They both mean 'knowledge,' but in different ways: *savoir* is knowledge of fact (or know-how); one can *sait que* ('know that') something is true. *Connaissance* is the kind of knowledge of a person, a 'knowledge of' rather than a 'knowledge that' or 'knowledge how.' It can never be a complete knowledge, and one cannot *connait que* ('know-of that') something is true. It is personal in character. An I-It relationship is not just true of magic; as I will discuss below under the heading of 'Science, Psychology, and Behaviourism,' psychology seeks a baseline *savoir* of people where it might seek a *connaissance* , and its theories are meant to be abstracted from relationships with specific people. Like magic, the powers that are based on science are epiphenomenal to the relationship science is based on. Relating in an I-Thou rather than I-It fashion is not simply less like magic and science; it is richer, fuller, and more human.

In the patristic and medieval eras, the goal of living had been contemplation and the goal of moral instruction was to conform people to reality. Now there was a shift from conforming people to reality, towards conforming reality to people.[88] This set the stage, centuries later, for a major and resource-intensive effort to create an artificial mind, a goal that would not have fit well with a society oriented to contemplation. This is not to say that there is no faith today, nor that there was no technology in the middle ages, nor that there has been no shift between the early modern period and today. Rather, it is to say that a basic trajectory was established in magic that significantly shapes science today.

The difference between the Renaissance magus and the mediaeval member of the Church casts a significant shadow today. The scientist seems to live more in the shadow of the Renaissance magus than of the member of mediaeval society. This is not to say that scientists cannot be humble and moral, nor that they cannot hold wonder at what they study. But it is to say that there are a number of points of contact between the Renaissance magus's way of relating to the world and that of a scientist and those who live in science's shadow. Governments today consult social scientists before making policy decisions: the relationship seems to be how to best deal with material rather than a relationship as to one's mother. We have more than a hint of secularised magic in which substantial fragments of Renaissance and early modern magic have long outlived some magical practices.

Under the patristic and medieval conception, this life was an apprenticeship to the life in Heaven, the beginning of an eternal glory contemplating God. Magic retained a sense of supernatural reality and a larger world, but its goal was to improve this life, understood as largely self-contained and not as beginning of the next. That was the new chief end of humanity. That shift is a shift towards the secular, magical as its beginning may be. Magic contains the seeds of its own secularisation, in other words of its becoming scientific. The shift from contemplation of the

[88] Lewis 1943, 46.

next world to power in this world is why the occult was associated with all sorts of Utopian visions to transform the world, a legacy reflected in our political ideologies. One of the tools developed in that magical milieu was science: a tool that, for Darwinian reasons, was to eclipse all the rest. The real magic that has emerged is science.

Science, Psychology, and Behaviourism

What is the niche science has carved out for itself? I'd like to look at an academic discipline that is working hard to be a science, psychology. I will more specifically look at behaviourism, as symptomatic within the history of psychology. Is it fair to look at behaviourism, which psychology itself rejected? It seems that behaviourism offers a valuable case study by demonstrating what is more subtly present elsewhere in psychology. Behaviourism makes some basic observations about reward and punishment and people repeating behaviours, and portrays this as a comprehensive psychological theory: behaviourism does not acknowledge beliefs, for instance. Nonetheless, I suggest that behaviourism is a conceivable development in modern psychology which would have been impossible in other settings. Behaviourism may be unusual in the extreme simplicity of its vision and its refusal to recognise internal states, but not in desiring a Newton who will make psychology a full-fledged science and let psychology know its material with the same kind of knowing as physics has for its material.

Newton and his kin provided a completely de-anthropomorphised account of natural phenomena, and behaviourism provided a de-anthropomorphised account of humans. In leading behaviourist B.F. Skinner's *Walden Two* (1948), we have a Utopian vision where every part of society seems to work better: artists raised under Skinner's

conditioning produce work which is 'extraordinarily good,'
the women are more beautiful,[89] and Skinner's alter ego
expresses the hope of controlling the weather,[90] and
compares himself with God.[91] Skinner seems to resemble a
Renaissance magus more than a mediaeval member: society
is raw material for him to transform. Skinner is, in a real
sense, a Renaissance magus whose magic has become
secularised. Quite a lot of the magus survives the
secularisation of Skinner's magic.

Even without these more grandiose aspirations,
psychology is symptomatic of something that is difficult to
discern by looking at the hard sciences. Psychological
experiments try to find ways in which the human person
responds in terms comparable to a physics experiment—
and by nature do not relate to their subjects as human
agents. These experiments study one aspect of human
personhood, good literature another, and literature offers a
different kind of knowing from a psychological experiment.
If we assume that psychology is the best way to understand
people—and that the mind is a mechanism-driven thing—
then the assumed burden of proof falls on anyone saying,
'But a human mind isn't the sort of thing you can duplicate
on a computer.' The cultural place of science constitutes a
powerful influence on how people conceive the question of
artificial intelligence.

Behaviourism offers a very simple and very sharp
magic sword to cut the Gordian knot of unscientific
teleology, a knot that will be discussed under the heading of
'Intentionality and Teleology' below. It removes suspicion of
the reason being attached to a spiritual intellect by refusing
to acknowledge reason. It removes the suspicion of
emotions having a spiritual dimension by refusing to
acknowledge emotions. He denies enough of the human
person that even psychologists who share those goals would

[89] *Ibid.*, 33-35.
[90] *Ibid.*, 23-24.
[91] *Ibid.*, 295-299.

want to distance themselves from him. And yet Skinner
does more than entertain messianic fantasies: *Walden Two*
is a Utopia, and when Skinner's alter ego compares himself
with God, God ends up second best.[92] I suggest that this is
no a contradiction at all, or more properly it is a blatant
contradiction as far as common sense is concerned, but as
far as human human phenomena go, we have two sides of
the same coin. The magic sword and the messianic fantasy
belong to one and the same magus.

There is in fact an intermediate step between the full-
fledged magus and the mortal herd. One can be a magician's
assistant, clearing away debris and performing menial tasks
to support the real magi.[93] The proportion of the Western
population who are scientists is enormous compared to
science's founding, and the vast majority of the increase is
in magician's assistants. If one meets a scientist at a social
gathering, the science is in all probability not a full-fledged
magus, but a magician's assistant, set midway between the
magus and the commoner. The common scientist is below
the magus in knowledge of science but well above most
commoners. In place of a personal messianic fantasy is a
more communal tendency to assume that the scientific
enterprise is our best hope for the betterment of society.
(Commoners may share this belief.) There is a significant
difference between the magus and most assistants today.
Nonetheless, the figure of the magus is alive today—
secularised, in most cases, but alive and well. Paul
Johnson's Augustinian account of *Intellectuals* includes
such eminent twentieth century scientific figures as
Bertrand Russell, Noam Chomsky, and Albert Einstein;[94]
the figures one encounters in his pages are steeped in the
relationship to society as to raw material instead as to one's
mother, the magic sword, and the messianic fantasy.

[92] *Ibid.*
[93] See Midgley, 1992, 80.
[94] 1990, 195, 197-224;337-41.

I-Thou and Humanness

I suggest that the most interesting critiques of artificial intelligence are not obtained by looking through I-It eyes in another direction, but in using other eyes to begin with, looking through I-Thou eyes. Let us consider Turing's 'Arguments from Various Disabilities'.[95][43] Perhaps the people who furnished Turing with these objections were speaking out of something deeper than they could explain:

> Be kind, resourceful, beautiful, friendly, have initiative, have a sense of humour, tell right from wrong, make mistakes, fall in love, enjoy strawberries and cream, make some one fall in love with it, learn from experience, use words properly, be the subject of its own thought, have as much diversity of behaviour as a man, do something really new.

Be kind:
Kindness is listed by Paul as the fruit of the Spirit (Gal. 5:22) in other words, an outflow of a person living in the Spirit. Disregarding the question of whether all kindness is the fruit of the Spirit, in humans kindness is not merely following rules, but the outflow of a concern for the other person. Even counterfeit kindness is a counterfeit from someone who knows the genuine article. It thus uses some faculty of humanity other than the reasoning ability, which classical AI tries to duplicate and which is assumed to be the one thing necessary to duplicate human cognition.

Be **resourceful:**
The artificial intelligence assumption is that if something is non-deterministic, it is random, because deterministic and pseudo-random are the only options one can use in

[95] 1950.

programming a computer. This leaves out a third possibility, that by non-computational faculties someone may think, not merely 'outside the box,' in a random direction, but above it. The creative spark comes neither from continuing a systematic approach, nor simply picking something random ('because I can't get my computer to turn on, I'll pour coffee on it and see if that helps'), but something that we don't know how to give a computer.

Be **beautiful:**

Beauty is a spiritual quality that is not perceived by scientific enquiry and, given our time's interpretation of scientific enquiry, is in principle not recognised. Why not? If we push materialist assumptions to the extreme, it is almost a category error to look at a woman and say, 'She is beautiful.' What is really being said—if one is not making a category error—is, 'I have certain emotions when I look at her.' Even if there is not a connection between physical beauty and intelligence, there seems to be some peasant shrewdness involved. It is a genuine, if misapplied, appeal to look at something that has been overlooked.

Be **friendly:**

True as opposed to counterfeit friendliness is a manifestation of love, which has its home in the will, especially if the will is not understood as a quasi-muscular power of domination, but part of the spirit which lets us turn towards another in love.

Remarks could easily be multiplied. What is meant to come through all this is that science is not magic, but science works in magic's wake. Among relevant features may be mentioned relating as a magus would (in many ways distilling an I-It relationship further), and seeking power over the world in this life rather living an apprenticeship to the next.

Orthodox Anthropology in Maximus Confessor's *Mystagogia*

I will begin detailed enquiry in the Greek Fathers by considering an author who is foundational to Eastern Orthodoxy, the seventh century Greek Father Maximus Confessor. Out of the existing body of literature, I will focus on one work, his *Mystagogia*,[96] with some reference to the *Capita Gnosticae*. Maximus Confessor is a synthetic thinker, and the *Mystagogia* is an anthropological work; its discussion of Church mystagogy is dense in theological anthropology as the training for a medical doctor is dense in human biology.

Orthodox Christians have a different cosmology from the Protestant division of nature, sin, and grace. Nature is never un-graced, and the grace that restores from sin is the same grace that provides continued existence and that created nature in the first place. That is to say, grace flows from God's generosity, and is never alien to nature. The one God inhabits the whole creation: granted, in a more special and concentrated way in a person than in a rock, but the same God is really present in both.

Already, without having seriously engaged theological *anthropology*, we have differences with how AI looks at things. Not only are the answers different, but the questions themselves are posed in a different way. 'Cold matter,' such as is assumed by scientific materialism, doesn't exist, not because matter is denied in Berkeleyan fashion but because it is part of a spiritual cosmology and affirmed to be something more. It is mistaken to think of cold matter, just as it is mistaken to think of tepid fire. Even

---

[96] References will be to the online Greek version at *Thesaurus Linguae Graecae*, http://stephanus.tlg.uci.edu/inst/wsearch?wtitle=2892+049&uid= &GreekFont=Unicode&mode=c_search, according to chapter and line. Unless otherwise specified, references in this section will be to the *Mystagogia*.

matter has spiritual attributes and is graced. Everything that exists, from God and the spiritual creation to the material creation, from seraphim to stone, is the sort of thing one connects to in an I-Thou relationship. An I-It relationship is out of place, and from this perspective magic and science look almost the same, different signposts in the process of establishing a progressively purer I-It relationship.

Intellect and Reason

Maximus' anthropology is threefold: the person is divided into soul and body, and the soul itself is divided into a higher part, the intellect, and a lower part, the reason:[97]

> [Pseudo-Dionysius] used to teach that the whole person is a synthesis of soul and body joined together, and furthermore the soul itself can be examined by reason. (The person is an image which reflects teaching about the Holy Church.) Thus he said that the soul had an intellectual and living faculty that were essentially united, and described the moving, intellectual, authoritative power—with the living part described according its will-less nature. And again, the whole mind deals with intelligible things, with the intelligible power being called intellect, whilst the sensible power is called reason.

[97] 5.1-10. 'Intellect' in particular is used as a scholarly rendering of the Greek '*nous*,' and is not equivalent to the layman's use of 'intellect,' particularly not as cognate to 'intelligence.' The 'reason' ('*logos*') is closer to today's use of the term, but not as close as you might think. This basic conceptualisation is common to other patristic and medieval authors, such as Augustine.

This passage shows a one-word translation difficulty which is symptomatic of a difference between his theology and the quasi-theological assumptions of the artificial intelligence project. The word in question, which I have rendered as 'authoritative power,' is '*exousiastikws*,' with root word '*exousia.*' The root and its associated forms could be misconstrued today as having a double meaning of 'power' and 'authority,' with 'authority' as the basic sense. In both classical and patristic usage, it seems debatable whether 'exousia' is tied to any concept of power divorced from authority. In particular this passage's '*exousiastikws*' is most immediately translated as power rather than any kind of authority that is separate from power. Yet Maximus Confessor's whole sense of power here is one that arises from a divine authorisation to know the truth. This sense of power is teleologically oriented and has intrinsic meaning. This is not to say that Maximus could only conceive of power in terms of authority. He repeatedly uses '*dunamis*,' (*proem*.15-6, 26, 28, etc), a word for power without significant connotations of authority. However, he could conceive of power in terms of authority, and that is exactly what he does when describing the intellect's power.

What is the relationship between 'intellect'/'reason' and cognitive faculties? Which, if either, has cognitive faculties a computer can't duplicate? Here we run into another difficulty. It is hard to say that Maximus Confessor traded in cognitive faculties. For Maximus Confessor the core sense of 'cognitive faculties' is inadequate, as it is inadequate to define an eye as something that provides nerve impulses which the brain uses to generate other nerve impulses. What is missing from this picture? This definition does not provide any sense that the eye interacts with the external world, so that under normal circumstances its nerve impulses are sent because photons strike photoreceptors in an organ resembling a camera. Even this description hides most teleology and evaluative judgment. It does not say that an eye is an organ for perceiving the external world through an image reconstructed in the brain, and may be called 'good' if it sees clearly and 'bad' if it doesn't. This may be used as a point of departure to comment on Maximus Confessor and the conception of cognitive faculties.

Maximus Confessor does not, in an amoral or self-contained fashion, see faculties that operate on mental representations. He sees an intellect that is where one meets God, and where one encounters a Truth that is no more private than the world one sees with the eye is private.

Intellect and reason compete with today's cognitive faculties, but Maximus Confessor understands the intellect in particular as something fundamentally moral, spiritual, and connected to spiritual realities. His conception of morality is itself different from today's private choice of ethical code; morality had more public and more encompassing boundaries, and included such things as Jesus' admonition not to take the place of highest honour so as not to receive public humiliation (Luke 14:7-10): it embraced practical advice for social conduct, because the moral and spiritual were not separated from the practical. It is difficult to Maximus Confessor conceiving of practicality as hampered by morality. In Maximus Confessor's day what we separate into cognitive, moral, spiritual, and practical domains were woven into a seamless tapestry.

Intellect, Principles, and Cosmology

Chapter twenty-three opens by emphasising that contemplation is more than looking at appearances (23.1-10), and discusses the Principles of things. The concept of a *Principle* is important to his cosmology. There is a foundational difference between the assumed cosmologies of artificial intelligence and Maximus Confessor. Maximus Confessor's cosmology is not the artificial intelligence cosmology with a spiritual dimension added, as a living organism is not a machine modified to use foodstuffs as fuel.

Why do I speak of the 'artificial intelligence cosmology'? Surely one can have a long debate about artificial intelligence without adding cosmology to the discussion. This is true, but it is true because cosmology has become invisible, part of the assumed backdrop of discussion. In America, one cultural assumption is that 'culture' and 'customs' are for faroff and exotic people, not for 'us'—'we' are just being human. It doesn't occur to most Americans to think of eating Turkey on Thanksgiving Day or removing one's hat inside a building as customs, because 'custom' is a concept that only applies to exotic people. I suggest that Maximus Confessor has an interesting cosmology, not because he's exotic, but because he's human.

Artificial intelligence proponents and (most) critics do not differ on cosmology, but because that is because it is an important assumption which is not questioned even by most people who deny the possibility of artificial intelligence. Searle may disagree with Fodor about what is implied by a materialist cosmology, but not whether one should accept materialism. I suggest that some artificial intelligence critics miss the most interesting critiques of artificial intelligence because they share that project's cosmology. If AI is based on a cosmological error, then no amount of fine-tuning within the system will rectify the error. We need to consider cosmology if we are to have any hope of correcting an error that basic. (Bad metaphysics does not create good physics.) I will describe Maximus Confessor's cosmology in this section, not because he has cosmology and AI doesn't, but because his cosmology seems to suggest a correction to the artificial intelligence cosmology.

At the base of Maximus's cosmology is God. God holds the Principles in his heart, and they share something of his reality. Concrete beings (including us) are created through the Principles, and we share something of their reality and of God. The Principles are a more concrete realisation of God, and we are a more concrete realisation of the Principles. Thought (*nohsis*) means beholding God and the Principles (*logoi*) through the eye of the intellect. Thinking of a tree means connecting with something that is more tree-like than the tree itself.

It may be easier to see what the important Principles in Maximus Confessor's cosmology if we see how they are being dismantled today. Without saying that Church Fathers simply grafted in Platonism, I believe it safe to say that Plato resembled some of Church doctrine, and at any rate Plato's one finger pointing up to God offers a closer approximation to Christianity than Aristotle's fingers pointing down. I would suggest further that looking at Plato can suggest how Christianity differs from Aristotelianism's materialistic tendencies, tendencies that are still unfolding today. Edelman describes the assumptions accompanying Darwin's evolution as the 'death blow' to the essentialism, the doctrine that there are fixed kinds of things, as taught by Plato and other idealists.[98] Edelman seems not to appreciate why so many biologists assent to punctuated equilibrium.[99] However, if we assume that there is solid evidence establishing that all life gradually evolved from a common ancestor, then this remark is both apropos and perceptive.

When we look around, we see organisms that fit neatly into different classes: human, housefly, oak. Beginning philosophy students may find it quaint to hear of

---

[98] 1992, 239.

[99] 'Punctuated equilibrium' is a variant on Darwin's theory of (gradual) evolution. It tries to retain an essentially Darwinian mechanism whilst acknowledging a fossil record and other evidence which indicate long periods of stability interrupted by the abrupt appearance and disappearance of life forms. It is called 'punk eek' by the irreverent.

Plato's Ideas, and the Ideal horse that is copied in all physical horses, but we tend to assume Platonism at least in that horses are similar 'as if' there were an Ideal horse: we don't believe in the Ideal horse any more, but we still treat its shadow as if it were the Ideal horse's shadowy copy.

Darwin's theory of evolution suggests that all organisms are connected via slow, continuous change to a common ancestor and therefore to each other. If this is true, there are dire implications for Platonism. It is as if we had pictures of wet clay pottery, and posited a sharp divide between discrete classes of plates, cups, and bowls. Then someone showed a movie of a potter deforming one and the same clay from one shape to another, so that the divisions are now shown to be arbitrary. There are no discrete classes of vessels, just one lump of clay being shaped into different things. Here we are pushing a picture to the other end of a spectrum, further away from Platonism. It is a push from tacitly assuming there is a shadow, to expunging the remnant of belief in the horse and its shadow.

But this doesn't mean we're perfect Platonists, or can effortlessly appreciate the Platonic mindset. There are things we have to understand before we can travel in the other direction. If anything, there is more work involved. We act as if the Ideas' shadows are real things, but we don't genuinely believe in the shadows *qua* shadows, let alone the Ideas. We've simply inherited the habit of treating shadows as a convenient fiction. But Maximus Confessor believed the Principles (Ideas) represented something fuller and deeper than concrete things.

This is foundational to why Maximus Confessor would not have understood thought as manipulating mental representations in the inescapable privacy of one's mind. Contemplation is not a matter of closing one's eyes and fantasising, but of opening one's eyes and beholding something deeper and more real than reality itself. The sensible reason can perceive the external physical world through the senses, but this takes a very different light from Kant's view.

Maximus Confessor offers a genuinely interesting suggestion that we know things not only because of our power-to-know, but because of their power-to-be-known, an approach that I will explore later under the heading 'Knowledge of the Immanent.' The world is not purely transcendent, but immanent. For Kant the mind is a box that is hermetically sealed on top but has a few frustratingly small holes on the bottom: the senses. Maximus Confessor doesn't view the senses very differently, but the top of the box is open.

This means that the intellect is most basically where one meets God. Its powerful ability to know truth is connected to this, and it connects with the Principles of things, as the senses connect with mere things. Is it fair to the senses to compare the intellect's connection with Principles with the senses' experience of physical things? The real question is not that, but whether it is fair to the intellect, and the answer is 'no.' The Principles are deeper, richer, and fuller than the mere visible things, as a horse is richer than its shadow. The knowledge we have through the intellect's connection with the Principles is of a deeper and richer sort than what is merely inferred from the senses.

The Intelligible and the Sensible

Maximus Confessor lists, and connects, several linked pairs, which I have incorporated into a schema below. The first column of this schema relates to the second column along lines just illustrated: the first member of each pair is transcendent and eminent to the second, but also immanent to it.

Head	Body
Heaven	earth (3.1-6)

Head	Body
holy of holies	sanctuary (2.8-9)
intelligible	sensible (7.5-10)
contemplative	active (5.8-9)
intellect	reason (5.9-10)
spiritual wisdom	practical wisdom (5.13-15)
knowledge	virtue (5.58)
unforgettable knowledge	faith (5.58-60)
truth	goodness (5.58-9)
archetype	image (5.79-80)
New Testament	Old Testament (6.4-6)
spiritual meaning of a text	literal meaning of a text (6.14-5)
bishop's seating on throne	bishop's entrance into Church (8.5-6, 20-21)
Christ's return in glory	Christ's first coming, glory veiled (8.6-7, 18)

Maximus Confessor's cosmology sees neither a disparate collection of unconnected things, nor an undistinguished monism that denies differences. Instead, he sees a unity that sees natures (1.16-17) in which God not only limits differences, as a circle limits its radii (1.62-67), but transcends all differences. Things may be distinguished, but they are not divided. This is key to understanding both doctrine and method. He identifies the world with a person, and connects the Church with the image of God. Doctrine and method are alike synthetic, which suggests that passages about his cosmology and ecclesiology illuminate anthropology.

One recurring theme shows in his treatment of heaven and earth, the soul and the body, the intelligible (spiritual) and the sensible (material). The intelligible both transcends the sensible, and is immanent to it, present in it. The intelligible is what can be apprehended by the part of us that meets God; the sensible is what presents itself to the world of senses. (The senses are not our only connection with the world.) This is a different way of thinking about matter and spirit from the Cartesian model, which gives rise to the ghost in the machine problem. Maximus Confessor's understanding of spirit and matter does not make much room for this dilemma. Matter and spirit interpenetrate. This is true not just in us but in the cosmos, which is itself 'human': he considers '...the three people: the cosmos (let us say), the Holy Scriptures, and this is true with us' (7.40-1). The attempt to connect spirit and matter might have struck him like an attempt to forge a link between fire and heat, two things already linked.

Knowledge of the Immanent

The word which I here render 'thought' is '*nohsis*', cognate to 'intellect' ('*nous*') which has been discussed as that which is inseparably the home of thought and of meeting God. We already have a hint of a conceptual cast in which thought will be understood in terms of connection and contemplation.

In contrast to understanding thought as a process within a mind, Maximus describes thought in terms of a relationship: a thought can exist because there is a power to think of in the one thinking, and a power to be thought of in what is thought of.[100] We could no more know an absolutely transcendent creature than we could know an absolutely transcendent Creator. Even imperfect thought exists because we are dealing with something that 'holds power to be apprehended by the intellect' (I.82). We say something is purple because its manifest purpleness meets our ability to perceive purple. What about the claim that purple is a mental experience arising from a certain wavelength of light striking our retinas? One answer that might be given is that those are the mechanisms by which purple is delivered, not the nature of what purple is.[101] The distinction is important.

We may ask, what about capacity for fantasy and errors? The first response I would suggest is cultural. The birth of modernity was a major shift, and its abstraction introduced new things into the Western mind, including much of what supports our concept of fantasy (in literature, etc.). The category of fantasy is a basic category to our mindset but not to the patristic or medieval mind. Therefore, instead of speculating how Maximus Confessor would have replied to these objections, we can point out that they aren't the sort of thing that he would ever think of, or perhaps even understand.

But in fact a more positive reply can be taken. It can be said of good and evil that good is the only real substance. Evil is not its own substance, but a blemish in good substance. This parallels error. Error is not something fundamentally new, but a blurred or distorted form of truth. Fantasy does not represent another fundamentally independent, if hypothetical, reality; it is a funhouse mirror refracting this world. We do not have a representation that exists in one's mind alone, but a dual relationship that arises both from apprehending intellect and an immanent

[100] I.82. Material from the *Capita Gnosticae*, not available in *Thesaurus Linguae Graecae*, will be referenced by century and chapter number, i.e. I.82 abbreviates Century I, Chapter 82.
[101] See Lewis 2001, 522.

thing. The possibility of errors and speculation make for a longer explanation but need not make us discard this basic picture.

Intentionality and Teleology

One of the basic differences in cosmology between Maximus Confessor and our own day relates to *intentionality*. As it is described in cognitive science's philosophy of mind, 'intentionality' refers to an 'about-ness' of human mental states, such as beliefs and emotions. The word 'tree' is about an object outside the mind, and even the word 'pegasus' evokes something that one could imagine existing outside of the mind, even if it does not. Intentionality does not exist in computer programs: a computer chess program manipulates symbols in an entirely self-enclosed system, so 'queen' cannot refer to any external person or carry the web of associations we assume. Intentionality presents a philosophical problem for artificial intelligence. Human mental states and symbol manipulation are about something that reach out to the external world, whilst computer symbol manipulation is purely internal. A computer may manipulate symbols that are meaningful to humans using it, but the computer has no more sense of what a webpage means than a physical book has a sense that its pages contain good or bad writing. Intentionality is a special feature of living minds, and does not exist outside of them. Something significant will be achieved if ever a computer program first embodies intentionality outside of a living mind.

Maximus Confessor would likely have had difficulty understanding this perspective as he would have had difficulty understanding the problem of the ghost in the machine: this perspective makes intentionality a special exception as the ghost in the machine made our minds' interaction with our bodies a special exception, and to him

both 'exceptions' are in fact the crowning jewel of
something which permeates the cosmos.

The theory of evolution is symptomatic of a
difference between the post-Enlightenment West and the
patristic era. This theory is on analytic grounds not a true
answer to the question, 'Why is there life as we know it?'
because it does not address the question, 'Why is there life
as we know it?' At best it is a true answer to the question,
'How is there life as we know it?' which people often fail to
distinguish from the very different question, 'Why is there
life as we know it?' The Enlightenment contributed to an
effort to expunge all trace of teleology from causality, all
trace of 'Why?' from 'How?' Of Aristotle's four causes, only
the efficient cause[102] is familiar; a beginning philosophy
student is liable to misconstrue Aristotle's final cause[103] as
being an efficient cause whose effect curiously precedes the
cause. The heavy teleological scent to final causation is
liable to be missed at first by a student in the wake of
reducing 'why' to 'how'; in Maximus Confessor, causation is
not simply mechanical, but tells what purpose something
serves, what it embodies, what meaning and relationships
define it, and why it exists.

Strictly speaking, one should speak of 'scientific
mechanisms' rather than 'scientific explanations.' Why?
'Scientific proof' is an oxymoron: science does not deal in
positive proof any more than mathematics deals in
experiment, so talk of 'scientific proof' ordinarily signals a
speaker who has more faith in science than understanding
of what science really does. 'Scientific explanation' is a less
blatant contradiction in terms, but it reflects a
misunderstanding, perhaps one that is more widespread, as

---

[102] What we usually mean by 'cause' today: something which
mechanically brings about its effect, as time and favourable
conditions cause an acorn to grow into an oak.

[103] The 'final cause' is the goal something is progressing towards: thus a
mature oak is the final cause of the acorn that would one day grow
into it.

it often present among people who would never speak of 'scientific proof.' Talk of 'scientific explanation' is not simply careless speech; there needs to be a widespread category error before there is any reason to write a book like Mary Midgley's *Science as Salvation* (1992). Science is an enterprise which provides mechanisms and has been given the cultural place of providing explanations. This discrepancy has the effect that people searching for explanations turn to scientific mechanisms, and may not be receptive when a genuine explanation is provided, because 'explanation' to them means 'something like what science gives.' This may not be the only factor, but it casts a long shadow. The burden of proof is born by anyone who would present a non-scientific explanation as being as real as a scientific explanation. An even heavier burden of proof falls on the person who would claim that a non-scientific explanation—not just as social construction, but a real claim about the external world—offers something that science does not.

The distinction between mechanism and explanation is also relevant because the ways in which artificial intelligence has failed may reflect mechanisms made to do the work of explanations. In other words, the question of 'What is the nature of a human?' is answered by, 'We are able to discern these mental mechanisms in a human.' If this is true, the failure to duplicate a human mind in computers may be connected to researchers answering the wrong question in the first place. These are different, as the question, 'What literary devices can you find in *The Merchant of Venice*?'[104] is different from 'Why is *The Merchant of Venice* powerful drama?' The devices aren't irrelevant, but neither are they the whole picture.

Of the once great and beautiful land of teleology, a land once brimming in explanations, all has been

[104] As seen on the Project Gutenberg archive at
    http://www.gutenberg.net/etext97/1ws1810.txt on 15 June 2004.

conquered, all has been levelled, all has been razed and transformed by the power of I-It. All except two stubborn, embattled holdouts. The first holdout is intentionality: if it is a category error to project things in the human mind onto the outer world, nonetheless we recognise that intentionality exists in the mind—but about-ness of intentionality is far less than the about-ness once believed to fill the cosmos. The second and last holdout is evolution: if there is to be no mythic story of origins that gives shape and meaning to human existence, if there cannot be an answer to 'Why is there life as we know it?' because there is no reason at all for life, because housefly, horse, and human are alike the by-product of mindless forces that did not have us in mind, nonetheless there is still an emaciated spectre, an evolutionary mechanism that does just enough work to keep away a teleological approach to origins questions. The land of teleology has been razed, but there is a similarity between these two remnants, placeholders which are granted special permission to do what even the I-It approach recognises it cannot completely remove of teleology. That is the official picture, at least. Midgley is liable to pester us with counterexamples of a teleology that is far more persistent than the official picture gives credit for: she looks at evolution doing the work of a myth instead of a placeholder that keeps myths away, for instance.[105] Let's ignore her for the moment and stick with the official version. Then looking at both intentionality and evolution can be instructive in seeing what has happened to teleology, and appreciating what teleology was and could be. Now Midgley offers us reasons why it may not be productive to pretend we can excise teleology: the examples of teleology she discusses do not seem to be improved by being driven underground and presented as non-teleological.

Maximus's picture, as well as being teleological, is moral and spiritual. As well as having intentions, we are

[105] 1992, 147-165.

living manifestations of a teleological, moral and spiritual Intention in God's heart. Maximus Confessor held a cosmology, and therefore an anthropology, that did not see the world in terms of disconnected and meaningless things. He exhibited a number of traits that the Enlightenment stripped out: in particular, a pervasive teleology in both cosmology and anthropology. He believed in a threefold anthropology of intellect/spirit, reason/soul, and body, all intimately tied together. What cognitive science accounts for through cognitive faculties, manipulating mental representations, were accounted for quite differently by an intellect that sees God and the Principles of beings, and a reason that works with the truths apprehended by intellect. The differences between the respective cosmologies and anthropologies are not the differences between two alternate answers to the same question, but answers to two different questions, differently conceived. They are alike in that they can collide because they are wrestling with the same thing: where they disagree, at least one of them must be wrong. They are different in that they are looking at the same aspect of personhood from two different cultures, and Maximus Confessor seems to have enough distance to provide a genuinely interesting critique.

Conclusion

Maximus Confessor was a synthetic thinker, and I suggest that his writings, which are synthetic both in method and in doctrine, are valuable not only because he was brilliant but because synthetic enquiry can be itself valuable. I have pursued a synthetic enquiry, not out of an attempt to be like Maximus Confessor, but because I think an approach that is sensitive to connections could be productive here. I'm not the only critic who has the resources to interpret AI as floundering in a way that may be symptomatic of a cosmological error. It's not hard to see that many religious cosmologies offer inhospitable climates to machines that think: Foerst's reinterpretation of the image of God[106] seems part of an effort to avoid seeing exactly this point. The interesting task is understanding and conveying an interconnected web. So I have connected science with magic, for instance, because although the official version is that they're completely unrelated, there is a strong historic link between them, and cultural factors today obscure the difference, and for that matter obscure several other things that interest us.

This dissertation falls under the heading of boundary issues between religion and science, and some readers may perceive me to approach boundary issues in a slightly different fashion. That perception is correct. One of the main ways that boundary issues are framed seems to be for Christian theologians to show the compatibility of their timeless doctrines with that minority of scientific theories which have already been accepted by the scientific community and which have not yet been rejected by that same community. With the question of origins, there has been a lot of work done to show that Christianity is far more compatible with evolutionary theory than a literal reading of Genesis 1 would suggest. It seems to have only been recently that gadflies within the intelligent design movement have suggested both that the scientific case for evolution is weaker that it has been made out to be, and there seems to be good reason to believe that Christianity and evolution are incompatible at a deep enough level that the literal details of Genesis 1 are almost superfluous. Nobody conceives the boundary issues to mean that theologians should demonstrate the compatibility of Christianity with that silent majority of scientific theories which have either been both accepted and discredited (like spontaneous generation) or not yet accepted (like the cognitive-theoretic model of the universe). The minority is different, but not as different as people often assume.

[106] 1998, 104-7.

One of the questions which is debated is whether it is best to understand subject-matter from within or without. I am an M.Phil. student in theology with a master's and an adjunct professorship in the sciences. I have worked to understand the sciences from within, and from that base look and understand science from without as well as within. Someone who only sees science from without may lack appreciation of certain things that come with experience of science, whilst someone who only sees science from within may not be able to question enough of science's self-portrayal. This composite view may not be available to all, nor is it needed, but I believe it has helped me in another basic role from showing religion's compatibility with current science: namely, serving as a critical observer and raising important questions that science is itself unlikely to raise, sometimes turning a scientific assumption on its head. Theology may have other things to offer in its discussion with science than simply offering assent: instead of solely being the recipient of claims from science, it should be an agent which adds to the conversation.

Are there reasons why the position I propose is to be preferred? Science's interpretation of the matter is deeply entrenched, enough so that it seems strange to connect science with the occult. One response is that this perspective should at least be listened to, because it is challenging a now entrenched cultural force, and it may be a cue to how we could avoid some of our own blind spots. Even if it is wrong, it could be wrong in an interesting way. A more positive response would be to say that this is by my own admission far from a complete picture, but it makes sense of part of the historical record that is meaningless if one says that modern science just happened to be born whilst a magical movement waxed strong, and some of science's founders just happened to be magicians. A more robust picture would see the early modern era as an interlocking whole that encompassed a continuing Reformation, Descartes, magic, nascent science, and the wake of the Renaissance polymath. They all interconnect, even if none is fully determined. Lack of time and space preclude me from more than mentioning what that broader picture might be. There is also another reason to question the validity of science's basic picture:

Artificial intelligence doesn't work, at least not for a working copy of human intelligence.

Billions of dollars have been expended in the pursuit of artificial intelligence, so it is difficult to say the artificial intelligence project has failed through lack of funding. The project has attracted many of the world's most brilliant minds, so it is difficult to say that the project has failed through lack of talent. Technology has improved a thousandfold or a millionfold since a giant like Turing thought computer technology was powerful enough for artificial intelligence, so it is difficult to say that today's computers are too underpowered for artificial intelligence. Computer science has matured considerably, so it's hard to say that artificial intelligence hasn't had a chance to mature. In 1950, one could have posited a number of reasons for the lack of success then, but subsequent experience has made many of these possibilities difficult to maintain. This leaves open the possibility that artificial intelligence has failed because the whole enterprise is based on a false assumption, perhaps an error so deep as to be cosmological.

The power of science-based technology is a side effect of learning something significant about the natural world, and both scientific knowledge and technology are impressive cultural achievements. Yet science is not a complete picture—and I do not mean simply that we can have our own private fantasies—and science does not capture the spiritual qualities of matter, let alone a human being. The question of whether science understands mechanical properties of physical things has been put to the test, and the outcome is a resounding yes. The question of whether science understands enough about humans to duplicate human thought is also being put to the test, and when the rubber meets the road, the answer to that question looks a lot like, 'No.' It's not definitive (it couldn't be), but the picture so far is that science is trying something that can't work. It can't work because of spiritual principles, as a perpetual motion machine can't work because of physical principles. It's not a matter of insufficient resources available so far, or still needing to find the right approach. It doesn't seem to be the sort of thing which could work.

We miss something about the artificial intelligence project if we frame it as something that began after computer scientists saw that computers can manipulate symbols. People have been trying to make intelligent computers for half a century, but artificial intelligence is a phenomenon that has been centuries in the making. The fact that people saw the brain as a telephone switchboard, when that was the new technology, is more a symptom than a beginning. There's more than artificial intelligence's surface resemblance to alchemists' artificial person ('homunculus'). A repeated feature of the occult enterprise is that you do not have people giving to society in the ways that people have always given to society; you have exceptional figures trying to delve into unexplored recesses and forge some new creation, some new power—some new technology or method—to achieve something mythic that has simply not been achieved before. The magus is endowed with a magic sword to powerfully slice through his day's Gordian knots, and with a messianic fantasy. This is true of Leibniz's *Ars Combinatoria* and it is true of more than a little of artificial intelligence. To the reader who suggests, 'But magic doesn't really work!' I would point out that artificial intelligence also doesn't really work—although its researchers find it to work, like Renaissance magi and modern neo-pagans. The vast gap between magic and science that exists in our imagination is a cultural prejudice rather than a historical conclusion. Some puzzles which emerge from an non-historical picture of science—in particular, why a discipline with modest claims about falsifying hypotheses is held in such awe—seem to make a lot more sense if science is investigated as a historical phenomenon partly stemming from magic.

If there is one unexpected theme running through this enquiry, it is what has emerged about relationships. The question of whether one relates to society (or the natural world) as to one's mother or as to raw material, in I-Thou or I-It fashion, first crept in as a minor clarification. The more I have thought about it, the more significant it seems. The Renaissance magus distinguished himself from his medieval predecessors by converting I-Thou relationships into I-It. How is modern science different? To start with, it is much more consistent in pursuing I-It relationships. The fact that science gives mechanisms instead of explanations is connected; an explanation is an I-Thou thing, whilst a bare mechanism is I-It: if you are going to relate to the world in I-It fashion, there is every reason to replace explanations with mechanisms. An I-Thou relationship understands in a holistic, teleological fashion: if you are going to push an I-It relationship far enough, the obvious approach is to try to expunge teleology as the Enlightenment tried. A great many things about magus and scientist alike hinge on the rejection of Orthodoxy's I-Thou relationship.

In Arthurian legend, the figure of Merlin is a figure who holds magical powers, not by spells and incantations, but by something deeper and fundamental. Merlin does not need spells and incantations because he relates to the natural world in a way that almost goes beyond I-Thou; he relates to nature as if it were human. I suggest that science provides a figure of an anti-Merlin who holds anti-magical powers, not by spells and incantations, but by something deeper and fundamental. Science does not need spells and incantations because it relates to the natural world and humans in a way that almost goes beyond I-It; it relates to even the human as if it were inanimate. In both cases, the power hinges on a relationship, and the power is epiphenomenal to that relationship.

If this is a problem, what all is to be done? Let me say what is not to be done. What is not to be done is to engineer a programme to enlist people in an I-Thou ideology. Why not? 'I-Thou ideology' is a contradiction in terms. The standard response of starting a political programme treats society as raw material to be transformed according to one's vision—and I am not just disputing the specific content of some visions, but saying that's the wrong way to start. Many of the obvious ways of 'making a difference' that present themselves to the modern mind work through an I-It relationship, calculating how to obtain a response from people, and are therefore tainted from the start. Does that mean that nothing is to be done? No; there are many things, from a walk of faith as transforming communion with God, to learning to relate to God, people, and the entire cosmos in I-Thou fashion, to using forms of persuasion that appeal to a whole person acting in freedom. But that is another thesis to explore.

Epilogue, 2010

I look back at this piece six years later, and see both real strengths and things I wince at. This was one of my first major works after being chrismated Orthodox, and while I am enthusiastic for Orthodoxy there are misunderstandings. My focus on cosmology is just one step away from Western, and in particular scientific, roots, and such pressure to get cosmology right is not found in any good Orthodox theologian I know. That was one of several areas where I had a pretty Western way of trying to be Orthodox, and I do not blame people who raise eyebrows at my heavy use of existentialist distinction between I-Thou and I-It relationship. And the amount of time and energy spent discussing magic almost deterred me from posting it from my website; for that reason alone, I spent time

debating whether the piece was fit for human consumption.
And it is possibly theology in the academic sense, but not so
much the Orthodox sense: lots of ideas, cleverly put
together, with little invitation to worship.

But for all this, I am still posting it. The basic points
it raises, and much of the terrain, are interesting. There may
be fewer true believers among scientists who still chase an
artificial intelligence pot o' gold, but it remain an element of
the popular imagination and belief even as people's
interests turn more and more to finding a magic sword that
will slice through society's Gordian knots—which is to say
that there may be something relevant in this thesis besides
the artificial intelligence critique.

I am posting it because I believe it is interesting and
adds something to the convesation. I am also posting it in
the hope that it might serve as a sort of gateway drug to
some of my more recent works, and provide a contrast: this
is how I approached theology just after being received into
Holy Orthodoxy, and other works show what I would
present as theology having had more time to steep in
Orthodoxy, such as The Arena.

I pray that God will bless you.

Bibliography

Augustine, *In Euangelium Ioannis Tractatus*, in
Nicene and Post-Nicene Fathers, Series I, Volume VII,
Edinburgh: T & T Clarke, 1888.

Bianchi, Massimo Luigi, *Signatum Rerum: Segni,
Magia e Conoscenza da Paracelso a Leibniz*, Edizioni
dell'Ateneo, 1987.

Buber, Martin, *Ich und Du*, in *Werke*,Erster Band
Schriften zur Philosophie, Heidelberg: KÃ¶sel-Verlag, 1962,
79-170.

Caroll, Lewis, *Alice's Adventures in Wonderland*,
Cambridge: Candlewick Press, 2003.

Dixon, Thomas, 'Theology, Anti-Theology and Atheology: From Christian Passions to Secular Emotions,' in *Modern Theology*, Vol 15, No 3, Oxford: Blackwell 1999, 297-330.

Dreyfus, Hubert L., *What Computers Still Can't Do: A Critique of Artificial Reason*, London: MIT Press, 1992.

Edelman, Gerald, *Bright Air, Brilliant Fire*, New York: BasicBooks, 1992.

Fodor, Jerry, In *Critical Condition: Polemical Essays on Cognitive Science and the Philosophy of Mind*, London: MIT Press, 1998.

Foerst, Anne, 'Cog, a Humanoid Robot, and the Question of the Image of God,' in *Zygon* 33, no. 1, 1998, 91-111.

Gibson, William, *Neuromancer*, New York: Ace, 2003.

Harman, Gilbert, 'Some Philosophical Issues in Cognitive Science: Qualia, Intentionality, and the Mind-Body Problem,' in Posner 1989, pp. 831-848.

Hebb, D.O. *Organization of Behavior: A Neuropsychological Theory*, New York: Wiley, 1949.

Johnson, Paul, *Intellectuals*, New York: Perennial, 1990.

Layton, Bentley, The Gnostic Scriptures: Ancient Wisdom for the New Age, London: Doubleday, 1987.

Lee, Philip J., *Against the Protestant Gnostics*, New York: Oxford University Press, 1987.

VanLehn, Kurt, 'Problem Solving and Cognitive Skill Acquisition,' in Posner 1989, pp. 527-580.

Leibniz, Gottfried Wilhelm, Frieherr von, *Ars Combinatoria*, Francofurti: Henri Christopher Crockerum, 1690.

Lewis, C.S., *The Abolition of Man*, Oxford: Oxford University Press 1950-6.

Lewis, C.S., *That Hideous Strength*, London: MacMillan, 1965.

Lewis, C.S., *The Chronicles of Narnia*, London: Harper Collins, 2001.

Margot Adler, *Drawing Down the Moon: Witches, Druids, Goddess Worshippers and Other Pagans in America Today* (Revised and Expanded Edition), Boston: Beacon Press, 1986,

Maximus Confessor, *Capita Gnosticae (Capita Theologiae et OEconomiae)*, in *Patrologiae Graeca* 90: Maximus Confessor, Tome I, Paris: Migne, 1860, 1083-1462.

Maximus Confessor; Berthold, George (tr.), *Maximus Confessor: Selected Writings*, New York, Paulist Press,, 1985.

Maximus Confessor, *Mystagogia*, as published at *Thesaurus Linguae Graecae*, http://stephanus.tlg.uci.edu/inst/browser?uid=&lang=eng&work=2892049&context=21&rawescs=N&printable=N&betalink=Y&filepos=0&outline=N&GreekFont=Unicode. Citations from the *Mystagogia* will be referenced by chapter and line number as referenced by *Thesaurus Linguae Graecae*.

Midgley, Mary, *Science as Salvation: A Modern Myth and Its Meaning*, London: Routledge, 1992.

More, Thomas, *Thomas More: Utopia, Digitale Rekonstruktion* (online scan of 1516 Latin version), http://www.ub.uni-bielefeld.de/diglib/more/utopia/, as seen on 2 June 2004.

Norman, Donald, *The Invisible Computer*, London: MIT Press, 1998.

Norman, Donald, *Things That Make Us Smart*, Cambridge: Perseus 1994.

Von Neumann, John, *The Computer and the Brain*, London: Yale University Press, 1958.

Polanyi, Michael, *Personal Knowledge*, Chicago: University of Chicago Press, 1974.

Posner, Michael I. (ed.), *Foundations of Cognitive Science*, London: MIT, 1989.

Pseudo-Dionysius; Luibheid, Colm (tr.), *Pseudo-Dionysius: The Complete Works*, New York: Paulist Press, 1987.

Puddefoot, John, *God and the Mind Machine: Computers, Artificial Intelligence and the Human Soul*, London: SPCK1996.

Read, John, '*Alchimia e magia e la "separazione delle due vie"*,' in Cesare Vasoli (ed.), *Magia e scienza nella civilte umanistica*, Bologna: Societe editrice il Mulino 1976, 83-108.

Sacks, Oliver, *The Man who Mistook his Wife for a Hat*, Basingstroke: Picador, 1985.

Searle, John, *Minds, Brains, and Science*, London: British Broadcasting Corporation, 1984.

Searle, John, *The Mystery of Consciousness*, London: Granta Books, 1997.

Shakespeare, William, *The Merchant of Venice*, as seen on the *Project Gutenberg* archive at *http://www.gutenberg.net/etext97/1ws1810.txt* on 15 June 2004.

Skinner, B. F., *Walden Two*, New York: Macmillan, 1948.

Thomas, Keith, *Religion and the Decline of Magic: Studies in Popular Beliefs in Sixteenth and Seventeenth Century* England, Letchworth: Weidenfeld and Nicolson, 1971.

Turing, Alan M., 'Computing Machinery and Intelligence,' in *Mind* 49, 1950, pp. 433-60, as seen at http://cogprints.ecs.soton.ac.uk/archive/00000499/00/turing.html on 25 Feb 04.

Watts, Fraser, 'Artificial Intelligence' in *Psychology and Theology*, Aldercroft: Ashgate, 2002.

Webster, Charles, *From Paracelsus to Newton: Magic and the Making of Modern Science*, Cambridge: Cambridge University Press, 1982.

Yates, Frances A., *The Occult Philosophy in the Elizabethan Age*, London: Routledge, 1979.

Yates, Frances A., *Selected Works, Volume III: The Art of Memory,* London: Routledge, 1966, as reprinted 1999.

Conclusion

One previous parish priest said many times, "The longest journey we will ever take is the journey from the head to my heart."

These dissertations are in some sense reflective of a journey, starting with a place far from Orthodoxy, for the condition I started as a mathematician is far from the Orthodox heart. Up until the last thesis of the three, it is still a journey of the head, but a journey that had been captivated.

Still I hope that there may be something of profit in them, and that by contrast if nothing else some people may see the starting points from which I have tried to push further and further into Orthodoxy.

Discussion questions for "AI as an Arena for Magical Thinking among Skeptics"

1. How rational are the strong AI rationalists discussed in this work?

2. Is our sense of having 99% of psychology explained on materialist terms a good working model for the present?

3. What basic human intelligence is still not replicated by technology?

4. Were initial, founding concepts about what computers would accomplish still something now that we have seen what computers can do?

5. Can computers be useful without being able to achieve AI?